HOW MANY TIMES
CAN YOU SAY GOODBYE?

Living with bereavement

Jenifer Pardoe

HOW MANY TIMES
CAN YOU SAY GOODBYE?

Living with bereavement

A Liturgical Press Book

THE LITURGICAL PRESS
Collegeville, Minnesota

Cover design by David Manahan, O.S.B.

First published 1991
Triangle
SPCK
Holy Trinity Church
Marylebone Road
London NW1 4DU

This edition published for The Liturgical Press for marketing in the United States of America, the Philippines, Central America (excluding Belize), and Mexico.

Printed in the United States of America.

1	2	3	4	5	6	7	8

Library of Congress Cataloging-in-Publication Data

Pardoe, Jenifer.
    How many times can you say goodbye : living with bereavement / Jenifer Pardoe.
        p.   cm.
    Includes bibliographical references.
    ISBN 0-8146-2109-0
    1. Bereavement—Religious aspects—Christianity.   2. Consolation.
I. Title.
BV4905.P36 1991
248.8'6—dc20
                                                            91-39356
                                                               CIP

Contents

Acknowledgements

All books, like film award presentation ceremonies, have lots of thank yous at the beginning and this book is no exception. There are countless people whom I would wish to thank for training, helping, supporting, guiding and showing me some of the things I've tried to reflect in this book.

Over and above all that I want to acknowledge openly that every page of this book has been influenced by my work and conversations with my friend and colleague, Robin Pugsley. The responsibility for what is written is mine, any credit due is jointly shared.

Introduction

Margaret woke up cold. What had woken her? A noise? The dog hadn't barked so it couldn't have been that, because he didn't miss any strange sound. A bad dream then? Well no, she didn't really have bad dreams – oh . . . but that was before . . . she remembered. They were not really bad dreams, more an aching yearning pain that seemed to permeate her very being.

She reached out. There was the cold empty space in the bed beside her, the space where for over thirty years there had been a warm, reassuring presence. Her husband. That's what had woken her up. She was cold, very cold; not only in her body, but in her heart. Jack was gone; not away on business, nor even ill in hospital, terrible though that had been, but really gone. Dead.

Margaret shuddered, wide awake now, her heart racing, gazing through the shadowy darkness of her room, thoughts rushing through her mind. How could she manage to face another day? Another empty day with none of the jobs she had carried out day after day for so long that filled her time with things she enjoyed.

There seemed no point in running the home any more. Certainly the joy had gone out of it, and the part-time teaching job she did had proved too difficult to cope with just now. All that noise and energy from the children was too stark a contrast to how she felt: numb, disconnected, cold.

1

She shuddered again, remembering that the church pastoral visitor had said she would pay another visit that day. They meant well of course, but they were trying so hard to be sympathetic and reassuring, saying they would be praying for her. She wished they would go away and just leave her alone. But being left alone was so horrible too. Oh, she didn't know what she meant, she must be going mad, it seemed impossible to think about anything in a straightforward way. Yet she used to be so organized. Perhaps she was just bad. How awful, after all, to be wishing that people who only wanted to help would go away and leave her alone. How awful to be crying out to God, often out loud, in the middle of the night, 'How could you be so cruel?'

Yes, it must be that she was actually an awful person. It was the only explanation of why she should be left like this. That her husband should have battled with that terrible illness for so long, and then after all of that should have died. It was pointless and cruel. Her family were good, but a long way away and there was just no future at all. Maybe if she just stayed where she was and didn't answer the telephone or the doorbell, didn't let anybody in, if she didn't eat, then maybe she would die too – fairly quickly, and that would solve it all. There you are, she must really be an awful person, even to think such things.

Margaret pulled the duvet round her trying to get warm. Sleep was impossible now, yet she didn't want daylight to come. That meant facing another day. She gazed into the darkness, eyes dry and burning. If she could only cry it would help, but that seemed impossible too.

Many people will feel just like Margaret. The circumstances may be different: maybe it wasn't a husband who died, but a parent, a child, or a close friend. Maybe there was no death, but an accident affecting the personality, someone changed beyond recognition, or just drifted out of touch. It might be a relationship irreparably broken by force of circumstance or particular events: divorce, miscarriage, failure to come up to expectations.

All these experiences cause grief. Someone like Margaret, who feels so abandoned, has had a significant loss happen to them. She is bereft. Grieving is one of life's basic experiences, yet because of its intensely personal nature it tends to stay hidden, despite the amount of attention given to the subject today. People try to cope on their own.

This book is an attempt to look at some of the things that go on when people face a loss of someone or something significant in their lives. It is not meant to be a book with the message of 'here's how to cope.' There is no right way to handle grief. There is only your way, the way that feels right for you.

This book, then, tries to identify some of the common factors that can be found in different sorts of loss. It tries to point out that it is a common, though devastating, experience; that most people do survive it, but their lives are changed by it. There are no easy answers but maybe a few guidelines as to what might be happening, for Margaret, staring dry-eyed and forlorn into a new day, and for all the other people who have ever had that sort of feeling.

Part I

DEFINITIONS

1 · What is Grief?

For many Christian people who are caught up in the whirlpool of grief, the most difficult part may well be their realization that they are in fact feeling very distressed. Many Christians will say, 'If my faith was strong enough, surely, when someone dies, I should be full of joy for them. If I really believed then I would know they were in heaven, in eternal life, and I should be so glad about that. Why don't I feel like that? What *is* this that I feel?'

There are actually many reasons why people should feel so bad. What is this thing called grief? Can it be understood, explained, predicted? And if it can, does that in some way lessen the experience? This chapter looks at some of the components of grief and tries to explain how grief may be experienced.

First, though, we have to try to understand the ordinary human behaviour that we usually call 'normal'. For human beings to lose anything is a significant event. This is true whether the loss is small and relatively trivial or if total and of the greatest importance, such as losing through death someone we are deeply attached to.

Throughout any individual's life, relationships and feelings of being attached to a number of significant people are important for our good emotional health. From our very earliest days the sort of pattern of attachment we form with our parents or those that look after us will influence how we feel about any relationship later in life. Unfortunately, as is well known, in many instances the lack of strong attachment in early life can lead to significant difficulties later on. Overall, though, most individuals survive with a good enough attachment pattern established in early life, and from then on attachments and separations come and go as the span of life develops.

When we are at school, for example, we all develop very strong relationships with our peers and usually we also have one or two favourite teachers. These relationships assume great importance and for a period of time they are probably the most significant ones we have. But once we have left school and have gone on to a different sort of existence, those relationships cease to have anything like the same meaning. It is through patterns like this that most adults learn something of attachment and separation. It becomes an inevitable part of normal living that we form significant relationships with particular individuals for a period of time and then, often through force of circumstance, move away from those same relationships. However, what we begin to learn from this pattern is that as we move away from some relationships, we start to form others as part of a 'natural effect'; and so the cycle of attachment and separation continues in the pattern of our lives.

We usually have some warning when one of these changes is about to happen and we may also have the worry about this change balanced by the excitement that a change in circumstances often brings. We can anticipate good things happening. To follow our example through, leaving school is often a traumatic time: there is usually much regret but, on the other hand, there is also great excitement at the thought of doing new things and meeting new people at college or at work or wherever the next part of our life takes us. A balance is therefore established between what we are losing and what we are gaining, and this balance enables us to view our losses with a reasonable degree of calmness. We regret the end of our schooldays but look ahead to the future with great hope. Of course it must be said that many people can't wait to leave their schooldays behind and so not all losses are to be regretted. This is a point to which we will return later.

The loss of a significant relationship through death is, however, likely to be one that we have not been able to prepare for much in advance, and it is likely to be a loss that we do regret. This time it is not a natural parting of the ways like leaving school that has happened; rather, an unexpected factor, for example some form of incurable disease or sudden death through illness or accident has occurred, which propels us into a significant loss that we are not prepared for. In these instances our reaction to this great loss is likely to be much stronger, although it will have the same components of grief as any other unexpected loss.

Before moving on to discuss the process of loss in relation to the death of someone close to us, it is helpful to look at a less significant but nevertheless important and unexpected loss and see our reaction there. For example, it is unfortunately true that many people experience a burglary at their home; this usually means things being stolen and so a significant loss occurs. Sometimes these losses do not amount to anything important but more often than not they include the loss of some article of sentimental value which creates a strong emotional response. What sort of reaction are people likely to have?

First of all there is the inevitable sense of shock, what psychologists call denial: 'This thing hasn't happened to me, it can't be true.' Most people when they've experienced a burglary will spend some time, perhaps minutes, perhaps hours, trying to absorb what has happened to them. When it happened to me I just could not believe it. I had come home late from being with friends on Christmas Eve. When I opened the front door there were all my Christmas parcels strewn across the hallway in various stages of unwrappedness. It was actually obvious that a burglary had occurred but I refused to take it in. I remember thinking, 'Gosh, I didn't think I'd left all this out on the floor. Perhaps the family have arrived early and started unwrapping things!'

This is a very natural reaction to bad news. The defensive manoeuvre behind it is something like this: if I don't acknowledge that this thing has happened then I don't have to believe it is true; I won't have to understand what has occurred if I hold off from consciously realizing that it has happened. I can remember waiting some minutes before walking through the house, knowing that there must be proof of burglary at the back door, and when I got there in an uncomprehending state, lo and behold the kitchen door was broken right down! This, then, is the first stage of reacting to loss: denial – shock that something bad has happened – is our psyche's way of defending us from experiencing too great a sense of harm too quickly. The news is too difficult to hear, emotionally speaking, and so we block off recognizing the fact that the event has occurred.

After this comes a time of great anger and rage. To return to my burglary, I remember experiencing a whole flood of feelings. 'How could they do it on Christmas Eve, those so-and-so's! How cruel to be stealing presents obviously meant for children.' This reflects the feelings of 'Why is life so unfair?' 'Why should it happen to me?' Christians in particular have trouble with this part of the grief response because so often it seems that Christians are not meant to be angry – especially when the feeling is commonly directed towards God personally, as it were: 'I try to live a good life and see what He has let happen . . . I thought if you became a Christian only good things happened to you.' All these feelings reflect our helplessness when we are confronted with a loss of major importance, and it is interesting that although anger is one of the earliest parts of the grief process, people often deny it altogether.

Thirdly, anyone experiencing a significant loss will move into a time of yearning and searching. In psychological jargon this may be called bargaining. What is meant by this is that people begin to come to terms with what has happened. They are no longer refusing to accept the evidence of their own eyes but are hoping there may be some sort of rational explanation for what they fear is an irrational event. Hopefully they may at least be able to feel they have an element of control over what is happening. Back at the scene of the burglary, I can remember thinking next, 'Oh well, I suppose I can re-wrap some of the parcels that have just been torn open; I suppose I could use cash instead for some of the presents that have gone; there is some way that I can cope with this.' The most important thing to understand here is that people try to re-establish some sort of control over their situation. 'Maybe the circumstances aren't as bad as I first supposed; and if I do *X, Y* and *Z* it may be possible to redress the balance a bit and then I won't feel so upset.'

The fourth reaction is one of being depressed. The word 'depression' is used in a non-clinical sense, and maybe sadness is a better way of describing what is going on. Here the bargaining stage has given way to a period of time when you feel it is just not possible to cope with the situation and the future looks bleak. In response to the burglary my reaction became: 'Actually when I think about it and allow all the facts to sink in it is just too awful; there really is nothing I can do to pretend this hasn't happened. Christmas with the family will be a disaster and everyone will get upset; how ever will I tell them and whatever can I do?' It is a time of abject misery, when it just seems impossible to face the consequences of the loss that has occurred.

Again, it is important that this stage *is* experienced. So many people are frightened of being sad that they take medication to stop such feelings. Sometimes this can be necessary for a while, but for the process of grief to reach its conclusion, it does have to be experienced in all its stages.

Fifthly and finally, anyone reacting to a significant loss will come to a time of acceptance. The word 'acceptance' most emphatically does not mean that someone experiencing loss will get to the stage of saying, 'Ah, it's all over, it doesn't really matter any more.' Acceptance, as used here, means that people begin to absorb the experience into their everyday life so that it can be coped with instead of dominating their every thought. Initially it seems that every waking moment is filled with memories of the relationship that is lost. After some time though people begin to realize that they have spent minutes, hours, even days, without consciously thinking of the person who has died. Memories take the place of regrets so that they can become comforting things, whereas regrets usually emphasize the emptiness. The experience is not forgotten but is stored in memory.

To return to my burglary, it became possible to make alternative arrangements: to let family members know and to replace the presents with other things made available by other people or by just acknowledging that they would be replaced when the insurance money came through! It was possible to have a good Christmas, but a change had been forced onto us and it was different from what we'd planned. It did not mean the burglary was not talked about over Christmas lunch – it certainly was; it became part of the event, and is now alluded to as 'Do you remember when . . . etc. etc.' It became absorbed into my personal experience and my family's folklore, and life carried on.

Obviously when considering this process of loss we have to remember that an individual seldom goes through these stages as neatly as might seem to have been suggested. In real life, people's reactions are much more confused and muddled, but it is usually possible to see the patterns described, even though the individual's particular experience is unique.

So far we have looked at what happens when someone loses something significant. But are people's reactions the same when they lose *someone* significant? In essence they are. An individual will go through the process just as we have outlined it already. First denial: 'This thing can't have happened to me. He can't have died; he's in hospital; he's away on holiday, on business, he's always away working.' An individual will invent endless reasons why the absence of the person who has died is due to some circumstance that can change. It is temporary, not permanent.

Second, anger. 'How could he do this to me, how could he leave me all alone to manage, he promised me he would never leave me alone to cope by myself.' This sort of response can cause a great deal of guilt in people who discover they have such feelings. 'How can I be feeling sorry for myself, when I should be sad that he has died?' This is perhaps particularly true of Christians. But maybe it now seems a little clearer why people can truly believe in the resurrection hope for the person who has died, yet at the same time may still allow themselves to feel sad. We need to separate out these responses. A Christian can strongly believe in a triumphant entry into eternal life for the person who has died, but this does not mean that the people who remain on earth will not still deeply regret their passing. A fervent belief does not deny the existence of the human response: the two are not mutually exclusive.

14

Third, the bargaining stage. Here a bereaved person will often come to terms with the person's death by saying, 'Well he has physically gone, but he's still with me in so many ways. I will wear his clothes, I will not change anything in the house.' It becomes possible to feel that a compromise has been reached. The survivor can cope with the fact that the dead person may not be physically present, but feels that he or she is present in every other way. 'It isn't that he has totally gone away, it's just that I can't see him as I used to.'

Again it is possible to see that, for a Christian in particular, the responses can become muddled. The survivor will truly believe that their loved one has gone to eternal life, and although physically apart, will believe in being reunited in the afterlife. One can see how easily this vibrant statement of faith can become muddled with the emotional stage of bargaining that the person is not really dead.

This is the stage, sadly, when many people are ready to believe that they can be put in touch with the relative or friend who has died, and consult faith healers who make all sorts of promises. People's vulnerability at this time can be very great, and it is a poignant reflection on our society that there are many other people ready to prey on this. They have devious ways of making money from bereaved people's misery, whether by knocking on the door after a death, offering to clear the house for cash, including any objects of value; or by offering solace in exchange for cash or fees. It seems a reasonable rule of thumb that any genuine offers of help and support from people or organizations will be accompanied by a name and address, and a willingness to be checked out as to their motive in making contact. It is inevitably a part of the normal grieving process that people search for the dead person in a multitude of ways, but it is very necessary for friends of the bereaved to help them choose carefully. It can be one of the most helpful and long-lasting things that a friend can do.

This is the stage when the bereaved person often feels that the person who had died is with them in the house, talks to them, appears during the night, etc. Most bereaved people will talk of being quite sure they have seen the person who has died walking along the street and have called out to them before realizing that it could not be so.

Fourth, there is the time of sadness, which is usually understood as the classic presentation of grief. This is a time when the bereaved will say that there is no meaning in life at all. As far as they are concerned the future does not exist in any way, other than that they hope they won't live to have any part in it. Where there were plans for the future now there is just an aching void. It's the time when thoughts of suicide can be very common and this again is particularly distressing for people of strong faith. Certainly I have had it said to me by grieving, often very elderly, people: 'There's nothing left for me now, I just want to be with my husband. But he's a good man and he will be in heaven. If I kill myself, which is what I want to do because I can't bear this misery, then I will go to hell. Then I won't ever see him again. Whatever can I do?'

What an awful confusion of overwhelming feeling for someone well advanced in years to be coping with. Notice she said 'is' not 'was'. A comment such as this can indicate to a friend that the person is working out their grief very strongly but is still stuck on the question: 'Is he gone for ever or isn't he?' The main thing is not to point out the 'factual error' because for the person talking it isn't a mistake. It's an indication that they are working on it and what may seem to be an accepted fact one day can be vehemently denied the next as the bereaved person comes to terms with the loss.

Fifth, there is the period of acceptance, which can seem to be in stark contrast to the depths of despair of the previous stage. As we have already said, this does not mean recognizing that an individual has died, being quite able to cope with it and pretending it doesn't matter. It is rather that people can get to the stage of remembering some experiences, quite often the good ones, that were shared with the person who has died. Memories become bitter-sweet events in our lives that remind us of our grief but also of the pleasure of the relationship we had.

So far the process of grief that has been outlined is how people might react to the loss of someone they love, whether that person has died or has gone out of their life for good. The whole process can take some considerable length of time which is often underestimated. The period of time when acceptance becomes possible seems to link in with the first anniversary of events. It is at the time when someone can say, 'This time last year . . .'

The first anniversaries, birthdays, Christmas and other special events have been and gone and the grieving person has survived these especially difficult days. They now have a new experience of such days which starts a new pattern for the future. This does not mean that when the particular anniversary comes around next time the bereaved person will not find the day difficult. They certainly will. It will, though, be tempered by the healing gap of time, so that it has become 'This time the year before last . . .' not 'This time last year . . .'. It can be a time when a sensitive friend can make sure the bereaved person is especially thought of, so that they are not alone if they find it hard to be by themselves on those days. Or, alternatively, they are not pressured into social activity if they prefer to handle the day by staying on their own quietly, maybe visiting the grave.

After this, it seems that a period of acceptance might come, but probably only if those balances referred to earlier in the chapter are possible. It is certainly the time when the bereaved person begins to think about forming new attachments in various ways. Whether such attachments are possible will depend very much on how much help and support he or she has received whilst going through the process of loss (which we will be looking at later).

If this is a universal understanding of the grief process, how does the church assist the bereaved in the first stage of their loss, bearing in mind that many people who make little or no claim to Christian faith still look to the church to provide a fitting funeral rite?

2 · Faith, Religion and Ritual at Times of Loss

Although Christianity is the 'state religion' of Britain, it is often said that the majority of people who are nominally Christian will go to a church only on a very few occasions in their lives – for a Christmas or Easter service maybe, or a family christening. They will go to a funeral if someone in the family, a friend or a colleague, has died, but most of the people attending such a service will have little, if any, regular contact with their local church.

In this chapter we shall be looking at how this particular group of people might view and understand what is being offered to them by the church at the time of a major bereavement. We shall consider its three main functions: first to offer an explanation, based on the Christian faith, of the nature of death, understood as part of mankind's lot in a 'post fall' world; second, to demonstrate the love of the church by offering comprehensive support to the bereaved; and third to provide an easily available source of ritual which is necessary in any society for the public recognition and containment of grief.

For a Christian, death is the end of an individual's physical existence on this earth, but not the end of that person and his or her life's journey. Most Christians believe in an afterlife of some sort, often referred to as heaven, the place where the soul goes if the individual, when on earth, was a professed and active Christian. To some people this will mean having had a conversion experience and being 'saved'; for others it will mean having been baptized into the church. Over against heaven is hell, separation from God, and again there is a wide variety of views as to whether one has to be 'actively bad' or just unconverted to be in hell after death.

This is of course an extremely simplistic presentation of the after life but it may illustrate why many people, as they approach the end of their lives, are concerned to 'put their affairs in order'. Most people have absorbed the idea that there is some sort of accountability at the end of life and that they may well need to be preparing to 'meet their maker'. Whether they believe in heaven and hell as places that physically exist with a geography of their own, or as concepts existing on the spiritual plane alone, this view holds good. They feel the need to be ready to account for the direction their lives have taken.

Much of the church's teaching is based on a concept that implies the need to live 'holy' lives in this world, without expecting reward or recognition for it but anticipating that the afterlife will reflect something of the quality of this earthly life. It is not that people should be righteous in the expectation of some reward but rather they should behave righteously because of an inherent desire to do so. However this stance is often misunderstood by others who believe that Christians only 'do good work' to ensure a place for themselves in heaven.

This subject needs a great deal of careful study and thought but, with this outline, let us move on to look at the experience a bereaved person might have of the church when someone close to them has died.

The first thing that has to be done is to obtain a death certificate from a medical practitioner. Assuming for now that the cause of death is known and that there is no need for an inquest or autopsy then the death certificate is next taken to the Registrar for Births, Deaths and Marriages. This is of course traumatic in itself and involves an interview with the Registrar which we will discuss in more detail in chapter 11. At the end of this interview, amongst other things, the person registering the death will receive a piece of paper that authorizes the undertaker to be called to make arrangements. It is quite often the case that the person making the arrangements has not had to do this job before and so relies heavily on what he remembers from other funerals he has attended and on the undertaker's advice. In discussing arrangements he will be asked if he wants a clergyman to conduct the funeral service and most frequently the answer to this is yes. So here the bereaved person meets the church in action. Most people feel that the church 'knows about death', and that someone isn't really treated with proper respect and dignity at the time of their funeral unless the church is present. The undertaker then arranges this, maybe with the 'duty clergyman' at the nearest crematorium at the same time explaining that this involves a fee.

In my experience, even at this early stage when the process has hardly begun, the family trying to make sense of what is happening around them focus their general distress on what they see as the church's preoccupation with making money, rather than offering help. There is of course a much heard debate about the fees and the services of the church, with people

21

holding different views about whether or not there should be a charge for functions like funerals, but for the moment we are more concerned with how the 'consumers' experience the way the church's representative reaches out to them at their time of crisis. To a very recently bereaved family who are struggling with a multiplicity of emotions this early attention to fees can seem mercenary. Overall the cost of a funeral often comes as a big shock to people and the vicar's fees, peripheral as they are to the main bill, come in for lots of cynical comments like 'Even at a time like this, the church is making money.'

Once a member of the clergy has been appointed he or she will visit the home to make arrangements, if they have time, which many might not. This is a valuable time for the family to get to know the vicar or deacon and talk about the person who has died, but often the discussion will centre on practical arrangements like deciding on hymns, music, and order of service. This can again leave the family feeling at a loss. They are entering the strange world of the Christian church at a time of high emotional stress and may encounter what sounds like a foreign language. As it is, many Christians have trouble finding their way through the various orders of service and different translations of the Bible. For many others the choice of hymns is probably restricted to 'Love divine all loves excelling' and 'Away in a manger', neither of which, it might be thought, is very suitable for the occasion! The grieving family are very much in the vicar's care as to how they can have a funeral service that is meaningful and relevant both to the person who has died and to themselves.

In the book *The Shell Seekers* by Rosamunde Pilcher, one of the main characters expresses this trepidation well. Olivia, the daughter of the mother who has died, has arrived at her mother's home to make the funeral arrangements. She has contacted the village church and the vicar has agreed to call.

The Reverend Thomas Tillingham, vicar of Temple Pudley, called . . . Olivia did not look forward to the interview. Her acquaintance of vicars was slim and she was uncertain as to how they would deal with each other. Before his arrival she endeavoured to prepare herself for all exigencies, but this was difficult to do because she had no idea what sort of a man he was going to be. Perhaps elderly and cadaverous with a fluting voice and archaic views. Or young and trendy, favouring outlandish schemes for bringing religion up to date, inviting the congregation to shake hands with each other, and expecting them to sing new-fangled and jolly hymns to the accompaniment of the local pop group. Either prospect was daunting. Her greatest dread, however, was that the vicar might suggest that, together, he and Olivia should kneel in prayer. She decided that, should such a horrific eventuality arise, she would cook up a little headache, plead ill health, and dash from the room. But all her fears were mercifully unrealised. Mr Tillingham was neither young nor old; simply a nice ordinary middle aged man in a tweed jacket and a dog collar . . . Mr Tillingham got down to churchy business, the funeral would take place at three in the afternoon . . .

Obviously a great deal will depend on the ability of the clergyman to communicate in ways the family find helpful so that they feel they are central to these arrangements.

At the time of the funeral a set form of words is used and I think it is helpful to look at what sense these words can convey to this majority population who are not regular church attenders.

As the funeral party process into the church or crematorium the clergyman usually goes before the coffin reading words of Scripture. They are likely to begin as follows:

> Jesus said, I am the resurrection, and I am the life; he who believes in me, though he die, yet shall he live, and who ever lives and believes in me shall never die.

Two thoughts immediately flow from this preliminary verse to those unfamiliar with these texts: (1) so they believe in some form of ghosts then do they? and (2) but he didn't believe in God so what has happened to my husband? Words which are meant to be comforting and familiar may be frightening or threatening.

Then once the procession is settled in the church or crematorium chapel there will be other readings. They may include sentences like the following which are all taken from *The Alternative Service Book*, the revised, modern language prayer book.

> You turn men back into dust:
>   saying 'Return to dust you sons of Adam' (Psalm 90).

So it is with the resurrection of the dead. What is sown is perishable, what is raised is imperishable.

The sting of death is sin, and the power of sin is the law (1 Corinthians 15).

Having had the opportunity through working at a hospice of attending many funerals I have grown used to seeing the shudders and worried looks that pass between grieving family and friends as they struggle to make sense of the words being read. The symbolism is complicated and relies on a great deal of background information. Taken at face value the words sound sinister and can convey a false impression like some sort of second-rate horror movie. People receiving these words in a mood of sorrow, therefore, have little option but to shut out the emotionally distressing pictures that the words seem to convey. Again misunderstandings can occur, and the person leading the service and trying to communicate a Christian message may be hard put to it to demonstrate their true meaning.

If people are already ill at ease in unfamiliar surroundings the order of service becomes another pressure. When do you stand up and sit down? Do you kneel? What are these strange hymns being played that no one knows and that seem interminable?

After this comes the 'disposal of the body' with more frightening sentences:

Man born of a woman has but a short time to live. Like a flower he blossoms and then withers; like a shadow he flees and never stays.

25

We have entrusted our brother —— to God's merciful keeping, and we now commit his body to the ground: earth to earth, ashes to ashes, dust to dust; in sure and certain hope of the resurrection to eternal life, through our Lord Jesus Christ, who died, was buried, and rose again for us. To him be glory for ever and ever.

The theological concepts contained in these phrases are weighty ones indeed and have been the subject of fervent discussion for centuries. Their meaning is not easily grasped by those who have spent some time studying the Christian faith, and yet the church still presents these complicated extracts from the Bible and the *ASB* to people who may never have heard the name of God spoken reverently before, and who are searching for some germ of belief to help them understand the vacuum created by the death of the person they love. It is hard for them to find the relevance to their lives of the words that are being used.

In all fairness it must of course also be said that people who are familiar with Christian orders of service find this same collection of words extremely comforting and helpful precisely because they are familiar and mean a great deal to them. It is also true to say that the minister (man or woman) is central in ensuring that the funeral service is a memorable event for the family by helping them to begin to understand their grief in the context of the church's care for them. In many circumstances, even when a clergyman works extremely hard, the ideal involvement just cannot be reached. A colleague of mine, in an inner-city team ministry, which faces a thousand funerals a year, cannot be as personally involved as he would wish. So far, though, we are only talking about arranging a meaningful funeral service. If we are to consider effective follow-up of the family concerned as an equally desirable function for the church to perform, then we very quickly face up to a major logistical exercise.

So how can the church be effective in this situation? The same colleague mentioned above used to describe himself, when discussing the problems of his work, as a sort of insurance agent for the church or maybe for God. On his initial visit to the home of the bereaved he would feel that he had a very short time indeed to set out his wares and try and convince the family to buy the package. In the middle of this he was trying really to listen to the distress of the family and demonstrate something of the compassion of God at the same time. He said he felt he often failed and yet it was important to keep on trying.

For, in spite of all the limitations mentioned, the church does provide 'rites of passage' for mourners to begin to recognize their changed status as grieving people. It provides a lever for the grief process to begin as people start to recognize what is taking place. The facts before them are to do with people dying and being buried or cremated. The difference this time is that it is someone they personally loved and therefore it takes on an importance quite different from any event they may have witnessed before.

The presence of ritual at significant life events like these is all-important. In my work I have been involved with many families who have needed to arrange a funeral. Of this large number of people I have known of only a small handful of people who opted for a non-Christian funeral. The families choosing such an event put a great deal of effort into making the formal disposal of the body (which is what the job has become) as relevant and reverent as possible, and yet it seemed extremely difficult to achieve. To create a sense of occasion that is in keeping with the depth of emotion felt at such times is very difficult without recognized formalities and strong ritualistic content.

The church is one of the institutions of British culture that contributes to this. We shall be looking at the process of registering a death in chapter 11. One of the functions of that difficult process is to provide a ritualistic framework within which people can function. What we mean by this, is that at times of great stress we can all be overwhelmed by the experience and find ourselves 'at sea', not knowing what to do.

The existence of a 'done order of going about things', even though it may be strange to us, enables us to cope. We do not really have to think about what has to be done. There are recognized ways of doing things that ensure that the job gets done at a time when we are probably incapable of thinking things through carefully. Thus the church provides a format in the Christian burial service. This helps us, as individuals, to recognize the reality of the event that has occurred. We would not be attending a funeral service unless someone we knew well had died. We would not be taking time off work, making all kinds of out-of-the-usual arrangements, unless we thought it was important to go to the funeral as a mark of how we feel about the person who had died, and wanted to 'pay our respects'. The format of the church funeral service allows this to be done in a recognized, public, orderly and time-limited way.

Secondly the fact of a recognized way of doing things is an acknowledgement of the importance of the event. It is a commemoration and ensures that people remember the event because it was out of the ordinary, and special. An illustration of this can be found in the funerals of very famous people conducted with great pomp and circumstance. If the person is considered to have been of outstanding importance to the nation then days of mourning might be decreed.

Attention will be focused on the event staged to mark the death of the prominent person, and in essence this is little different from any of us being involved in the funeral arrangements for a family member or friend. In our case the scale is smaller but the point of the ritual is the same. It marks the event and the behaviour we all become party to, namely attending a funeral service, sending flowers, writing a letter of condolence, and whatever else it might be that helps us cope with the situation. We're helped to recognize what has happened through doing things that usually we do not do.

Third, ritual is important because it contributes to the way society maintains its rules and therefore to general order. Some of the legislation concerned with registering a death is more to do with fears of grave-robbing some 150 years ago than with the requirements of society at the end of the twentieth century. But those regulations do ensure that we, the populace, go about disposing of dead people in an orderly way. Put like this it seems extremely cold and unfeeling, but it must be said that if we were all to make our own arrangements without any order or form then chaos would quickly result. The church ensures that this concept of being part of the social order of things is adhered to. The church is the re-cognized agent of the state for carrying out funerals within a certain framework. Although, as we have seen, it is possible to step outside this framework, and find an alternative that seems to fit the life style of the person who has died better than a traditional church funeral, in practice it is extremely difficult to do this.

The role of the church in this aspect of the ritualiz-ation of recognizing the death of an individual is an extremely important and positive one. Yet, unfor-tunately this positive role so often gets lost in the way we have described earlier, with people just not un-derstanding what is going on around them at a time when it could provide them with so much support. People frequently end up disillusioned, and even hostile to the part the church has played, rather than finding it helpful. Yet much of what we have dis-cussed can be overcome with sensitivity and by try-ing to 'feel into' how the family and friends of the dead person are feeling. Perhaps we can offer a few pointers at this stage.

First, make every effort to know the person who has died, whether you are visiting as someone in-volved in the funeral arrangements or as a friend who is trying to help. Ask about the person who has died and talk about them. Get a sense of how they fitted into their circle of acquaintances and hear all the anecdotes and stories concerning them. The 'Do you remember when?' stories can be so important in getting to know the person who has died, in hearing about how he or she appeared to their surviving family and friends.

Second, we can do a great deal to explain what is going on within the funeral service – the symbolism, the words used, the belief that lies behind some of the things said.

Third, it can be helpful to use straightforward simple words instead of using 'church speak' which means little to anyone other than a regular church-goer. 'We rejoice that our brother has passed through the valley and is in the everlasting arms of the Saviour' might mean something to a Christian but it is difficult for anyone else to understand. Indeed, at the risk of causing offence, it must be said that in response to such a comment I have heard more than one distraught person say, with a puzzled look, 'is that a pub around here then?'

The church does have an important part to play at this significant stage in a family's life and can use this opportunity to meet with people in distress by offering hope. The church is part of a wider society and it is to society's attitudes that we now turn.

3 · How Does Society Define Grief?

The Mourning Process

When a close relative dies, anyone in a full-time job is usually entitled to 'compassionate leave'. In statutory terms this is often a period of just three days. As will be clear from all that has been said so far, it seems that this short time is barely adequate for the person concerned to have dealt with all the issues involved in adjusting to the death of a loved one. Yet this notion of compassionate leave is one of the indications we have of how society accepts the significance of having someone close to us die.

In a society where we spend so much money, time and effort in trying to attain immortality, by constantly eradicating the diseases from which a human being can die, it may be said that we find it more and more difficult to face mortality either in ourselves or in those close to us. I am often asked to lead seminars on a topic which has been chosen for me and has a title like 'coming to terms with our own mortality'. More than once this has been printed on the programme as 'coming to terms with your own *immortality*'. It seems that our collective wish for this state is so strong that we are quite unable to contemplate the opposite. So dead bodies are hygienically whisked away by undertakers within a very short time of the person dying, funerals are conducted in twenty minutes at a busy crematorium with a bizarre queue of other funerals waiting in an approach way, and grieving people are expected to be back at their employment in as short a time as possible. Those who have been bereaved will say that they do not know how to behave as newly-bereaved people. It feels to them that a major event has changed their lives and yet people around them seem to be wanting them to forget it and 'get on with things' as quickly as possible. Do people wear black any more? Are they expected to observe a period of mourning? If so how are they expected to change their lifestyle? How can they find out what is expected of them? – or maybe nothing is. In some cultures the mourning period is very clearly established with a beginning phase where the bereaved will be looked after by their families; and there is an equally important ending phase when the person is expected to stop grieving and get on with living. Gone are the days when your emotional state was indicated by the depth of black border around the edge of your stationery or by changing your clothes from black to mauve to grey. But what do you do instead?

In some cultures there are still some established religious and social rituals surrounding death that help all the bereaved have a better understanding of how they are supposed to behave at certain times. It is even clear how long they are expected to grieve before becoming involved in ordinary life again. There is a time when they are expected to be looked after by family, friends and neighbours because they are too overcome to cope by themselves. There is a time when people gather to say prayers and comfort the mourners. After a prescribed time there is another ceremony that marks the end of mourning and this also is extremely helpful to the bereaved person. It enables everyone involved to understand the process that is going on, it makes it possible for grieving people to be looked after for a while, but not to sink into a chronic mourning state, because everyone knows when it is meant to be finished, and when the bereaved people are meant to pick up their responsibilities again.

Our society too still has recognized ways of marking the change in status that has occurred for some people. When a wife becomes a widow, for example, there will be all sorts of social changes. On top of that she will find herself in a different group for pensions and income tax. But how does she show, without losing control and breaking down, that a major life crisis has taken place? Announcements in newspapers are often a way of communicating information and people write letters and send flowers in return. This is society's attempt to recognize what is happening and to institute a mourning process. It is less ritualized than it was a hundred years ago, but it serves the same purpose of recognizing the event.

There is a common expectation that mourners will visit the cemetery where the dead person's body or ashes have been interred for a recognized period of time, attending to flowers at the grave and generally maintaining contact with the memory of the dead person. In some cemeteries an annual or regular service is held to which all the families and friends of people who have been buried or cremated in the last year are invited. In some ways it serves the same purpose as having a service to recognize the end of mourning. It may be held at that important time of the first anniversary of the death, and is thus at the time when the people most bereaved may be thinking of re-engaging in life.

There are other ways in which people go about recognizing socially this significant event in their lives. Some people leave effects of the dead person around – the hat that still hangs in the hall, the bedroom that is not touched, the area of the house that becomes a kind of 'shrine' to the memory of the person who is dead. Very often a favourite photograph is enlarged and framed. All these things signal to those around that a very significant loss has occurred. Very often the chair in which the dead person used to sit most when they were alive, becomes a chair in which no-one else sits. To ignore this can cause great offence.

In *Lewis Percy* by Anita Brookner there is a vivid description of such a situation. Lewis Percy lived with his mother in an intense relationship. In the book, his mother dies, and his cousin Andrew with his wife Susan descend on Lewis for the funeral: 'Lewis's rage sprang from Susan's occupancy of his mother's chair, and, by extension, spread to cover the whole of her existence. He not only found her annoying; he found her entirely and mysteriously offensive.'

So far in talking of the bereaved, we have had most clearly in mind the spouse of a dead person. However at the time of any one person's death or loss through some other means there are likely to be a significant number of people affected, not just the next of kin.

4 · Who Are the Grievers?

Whenever someone has been ill in hospital and has recovered sufficiently to go home, usually the first question asked is 'Have you got a family?'. And in the ward meetings where ongoing care is likely to be discussed the social worker will always be asked, 'Who is there in the family who can look after Mr Patient?'

When such questions are raised it is always the kin family that people are thinking of. When there is information to give about a diagnosis of terminal disease, for example, it is always the statutorily determined next of kin who are given the information, regardless of how suitable they may be to cope with such information emotionally, and regardless of how involved in the actual care of Mr Patient they are. As an example of the difficulties this can cause, I was working with a 33-year-old woman who had a rapidly progressing terminal condition. She was living with her boyfriend as she had for the last eight years and the hospital team were quite happy to talk to him about the proposed care plan for her. Her parents, who lived overseas, came to visit and then stay. When they arrived the hospital team changed tack and referred to them about all matters with regard to the girl's care because they were the next of kin. The boyfriend, who suddenly was not allowed to be involved in these discussions at all, talked to his girlfriend and they were married by special licence.

The hospital team again responded to this change and now once more talked to the new husband and did not talk to the parents. Obviously this caused a great deal of distress for all concerned, not least the hospital team. How much easier and clearer it might have been if it had been possible to say that both parents and husband were equally concerned and that they might all talk together.

People do not all live in nuclear family groups. To be living in a nuclear family household means parents and dependent children (statistically speaking 2.4) with no other relatives or friends. Yet we know for example that one in four British households in 1989 were comprised of people living on their own and one in three families were single parent families. Predictive studies suggest that, by the year 2000, fifty per cent of all households in Britain will consist of single parent units.

Even if individuals do live in a nuclear family group it does not necessarily mean that their closest emotional ties are to be found there. Many people when they have something to discuss may prefer to take it outside their family group to an old friend or a trusted adviser. Christian people are often in this category, discussing issues that concern them within the trusted confines of their church fellowship or house group.

When thinking about the bereaved, this is the sort of network of family and friends it becomes even more crucial to identify and contact. As we have said, when bereavement care is thought of, it is usually the spouse that we have in mind as needing support, and indeed they are likely to be the ones asking for care.

If there are children involved people often express some concern for them, but it is unusual for the circle of care to extend any further.

Let us look at what happens in the nuclear family when Mr Patient dies. What other relationships did he have and who else might be grieving? Within the family Mr Patient was a husband, father, son, brother, uncle, cousin, nephew, grandfather, brother-in-law, and so on. He was also the main wage-earner, the decision-maker in the family, the arbitrator, the do-it-yourself expert, and only car driver for family outings.

Much has been lost by various people in many different ways. All the people involved in those family relationships will be affected to some degree or another depending on how strong (positively or negatively) the emotional tie was. Additionally, Mr Patient was a churchwarden, an employee, a neighbour and the secretary of the local football team, so many more people will again be affected to a greater or lesser extent, depending on the degree of their emotional involvement.

Many people at the church will be saying to Mrs Patient and her family, 'I do miss your husband, he was so good to me,' and whereas this makes the family feel warm it also makes them feel disturbed. What did he do for these other people and do they actually miss him more than they do themselves? In addition Mr Patient is very likely to have had one or two close friends, probably from some time back in his life history, who may be dramatically affected by his death, even though they may not be visibly there close by or apparently very emotionally involved.

In any situation where someone has died, it may be assumed that more people are likely to be significantly affected by the death of that one individual than may seem apparent. This is one of the main problems of providing bereavement support. The people who may need it most are likely to be the unrecognized ones, the ones who it is somehow felt do not have a 'right' to support, even if it is known that they are upset. Moreover, time and again there are 'hidden grievers' who bear their distress alone, feeling that no-one can help them. Often these are people who have had a fairly 'secret' sort of relationship, such as a lover or a homosexual partner, and who therefore feel they have to bear their loss alone, because no one knows that they have sustained one.

It is important that those who set out to establish bereavement services spend some time deciding who they are providing them for. It needs to be remembered that bereaved people stay at home. The very nature of their distress means that they are likely to be unable to go out and face the social whirl, at least initially.

All this adds to the difficulty of bereavement service organizers in reaching out to those who may be most in need of the care that can be offered. All of us involved in bereavement care need to work on thinking through some of these issues so that the services we offer can be effective. Very often the bereaved will not come to find us, but we may need to make the approach to them. It may, for example, be necessary to undertake more home visiting than is thought usual, at least until the time when the bereaved person feels more able to go out and face the world again.

So far, we have talked of the fact that many people, other than the lost person's next of kin, will be grieving. There is however another sense in which we are all grieving people, because at some stage or another we will have lost something or someone significant. We can be in danger of saying or feeling that bereavement is something that happens to everyone else, and that 'those people' need support, but we are perfectly able to manage on our own.

Returning to my burglary, for instance, I've described the process, but what did it do to me? Friends came and made my house safe and secure. They asked me to go and stay with them, away from the place where the burglary had taken place. I remember I said thank you but no to that offer. I felt it would be much harder to return to the house if I left it. Both the house and I felt so vulnerable. The next day, Christmas Day, I could not do anything, just sat around a lot of the time, lost in my own thoughts. I remember excusing this by saying that I was waiting for the police and that nothing should be touched until they had come. That was true, but it was also a time of shock, suspended animation. My emotional reserves had been depleted. If I sat still and did not do anything then nothing else could happen that I might have to cope with.

In retrospect, I was shocked, dazed, confused and not able to cope. This was for a short time only; I had suffered a significant loss, but not a life-threatening or total one.

A person bereft by permanent loss or separation feels this range of emotion multiplied many times. It seems as though the world is going on, everybody rushing about their daily tasks, but surely this can only be because they have not yet heard the news or else they too would feel emotionally paralysed. It is as though you see the world through a glass wall; everybody is there doing their usual things but there is no connection with you at all. Nothing involves you and you feel as though it never will again.

It feels as though you have gone mad. You find yourself doing the strangest things that can only be because you are no longer capable of doing the simplest tasks. You make a cup of tea for a friend who has called around to express their condolences only to find as you pour it out, that there is no tea in the pot. How could you be so stupid. You do not want to wash, eat, think, plan, cope in any way.

You feel as though you must have become very bad, because the destructive thoughts that keep coming to you are most uncharacteristic and not at all the sort of thing you usually feel. 'It's all right for them, why couldn't it have been their child who died?' 'If there was a God he would not have let this happen.' You want to shout, 'It's not fair!' And all of this can only be because you are very wicked indeed. It can't be normal to feel like this. The last place you want to be is in church. You cannot pray and you feel unutterably alone and desolate. This must be hell. You just want to be left alone to die. How wicked can you get!

A little further along the path you just feel numb. Nothing matters. It seems you've survived, goodness knows how, for really it would not matter if you did not. Mary's husband had died three months ago from cancer of the lung. Shortly before he died,

Mary had noticed that she had great difficulty swallowing food, had gone to her doctor and he had organized X-rays and tests at the local hospital. Mary had forgotten all about them. One day the social worker from the hospital came round to see if Mary was all right. The hospital was worried; they had written to Mary several times asking her to come to the hospital for the results of her tests. They wanted her to be admitted as soon as possible for treatment as it seemed she had cancer of the oesophagus. Mary said she really could not be bothered. It really did not matter to her whether she had treatment or not. Her husband had died and she had no wish to think about her own future. If they sent an ambulance she supposed she would get into it, but if they did not, then she would leave it because she did not have the energy to take herself to hospital.

Some time later the tears and sadness come, and you start letting yourself feel the separation that has occurred. New events, new people are cropping up, and it begins to seem possible that life can go on, but people can still say wounding and painful things. They can say 'time heals' or 'it's time you put the past behind you' or 'you can get married again' or 'you can have another baby'. All these things are often said to comfort but of course actually hurt very badly. You do not forget, another relationship does not replace the one you have lost. It may be different, but it is not a substitute. The experience becomes absorbed into the stage of memory, of bittersweet experience, but it is not forgotten.

We are all grieving people whatever our individual losses and gains. I'm writing this at the start of the war in the Gulf. Many people feel a sense of over-whelming loss, loss of safety and security, perhaps, at the news that is coming from that part of the world, and yet find themselves unable to absorb the import of what is being said. Again we can see the effect that loss has upon us, where the first stage is shock and disbelief, and an inability to take in the reality of what is being said.

We will look a little later (in chapter seven) at the effects that disasters have on people, but first we will turn to particular sorts of loss, and some of the group of bereaved people who perhaps need special consideration.

Part II

SPECIAL GROUPS

5 · Facing Anticipated Death

So far we have thought of the expression of grief as a process that takes time and needs the opportunity and space to be lived through. We need now to look at what triggers people into expressing grief, at what moment someone realizes that they have lost something. For some people this process begins some time before the person they grieve for has died. It may be at the time that they hear the person is going to die; it may be when they suddenly recognize that the person has become very ill; it can be at almost any stage when the threat of loss comes into their mind.

Some people live with a more or less permanent anxiety that this shattering event could happen at any time. They live with a constant dread of the telephone ringing because they fear it will bring bad news. Perhaps a common expression of this are the preparations people undertake when they are about to go on a trip. Many people make wills and leave instructions about things that are important to them because they have assessed the risk and feel that they should anticipate the future and their possible demise. It is not uncommon for people to say, 'God willing, I'll be here tomorrow'. Old people in particular often ensure each night before they go to bed that their house is tidy and their last instructions are by their bed in case they should die in the night and someone will have to find them in the morning. All should be prepared just in case. This element of anticipation of death is therefore one that affects us all if the circumstances warrant it or seem to do so.

Additionally, it is often said how difficult people find it to say 'goodbye'. They will put the moment off for as long as possible or refuse to acknowledge that it is coming along and then protest that they were not told. This sort of response can cause a lot of confusion for those around who perhaps do not share the same feeling. People who respond in this way have often had a difficult early life when they had separation forced upon them, maybe by a parent being hospitalized or going away or dying. As we saw in the first chapter, an adult with this sort of emotional history finds it very hard to deal with separation of any sort. This is so even if the relationship they are worried about is a very strong one or the parting they are anxious about is a very ordinary and short one.

The insecurities created by separation in the early and formative years take their toll in adult life. If young children, dependent on an adult for basic needs, learn that the adult does not always come back, then this has far-reaching consequences for them in their own adult experience. They carry the same fear that someone will not come back even though as adults they may have far more control over the situation. The insecurities remain because they were so entrenched at a very important developmental time when as children they were dependent and let down.

This very anxiety can unfortunately cause just the rift they dread because people around find it very hard to deal with the 'clinging behaviour' that often results from this worry about separation. Just as young children will cry and remonstrate or say 'don't leave me', so the adult may use just the same words or convey by their behaviour that this is their worry. This can become intolerable for those on the receiving end who can feel trapped and unable to do things on their own. It is difficult for them to understand the fear that is being expressed unless they share it themselves, when there will be a mutual clinging.

Anticipated grief through expecting to lose something can, then, be a very powerful emotion that again is very common and widely experienced. So what happens when family members or friends are told or understand that someone close to them is going to die? Having looked briefly at some of the background to anticipated grief and why it occurs we need to consider how it gets expressed when someone is expected to die.

Classically, when a person has a prognosis of terminal illness the next of kin will be given the information by a member of the hospital team who has been involved in the treatment of the ill person. This usually is one of the medical staff. Having given the information, the first question that generally gets asked is, 'How long, doctor?' Again we discussed in the first chapter a little of why such questions get asked at this stage. People are trying to make sense of the bad news they have received, and are asking all sorts of questions as a way of regaining control of a situation that has frightened and disturbed them. Now we are looking at it from the point of view of anticipating a loss which will trigger the grief response. The question is therefore asked with an implication attached to it of 'Do I have to start getting really worried now or do I have time to adjust to this bad news?'

People who have been through this experience will describe how angry they feel with the doctor when having asked, 'How long', they are told something like, 'We can't really say. It could be anything between, say, three months and two years.' A prognosis can necessarily be only an educated guess, but for the person hearing the answer, it is not helping this underlying question: 'Do I have to start grieving yet or is there time to get used to the idea?'

After this initial time of taking in the news and trying to deal with its implications comes a time of absorbing the message given and trying to act on it.

Relatives or friends will say that the dying person must have whatever they want. It is unacceptable to think of the person who is maybe dying wanting something that is not delivered. This feeling owes a lot to all the novels and films and to actual practice with condemned men being 'granted their last wish before they die', but it is also a strong expression of trying to anticipate impending loss. People feel something like this: 'If I knew I did everything I possibly could then I wouldn't feel so bad after he's gone'. And so exotic fruit out of season will be sought out because the patient fancies it, and other such fairly innocuous things bought.

At the other end of the spectrum family events such as weddings may be brought forward because the dying person says they want to live to see it. In my experience, young people in a family have been directed to go and conceive a child as quickly as possible because a dying person wants to see a grand-child to 'know that his name will live on before he dies'. This sort of request has extremely complicated emotional, practical and social repercussions for the people who are left. The anticipated sense of loss can be so strong and the wish to feel you have done everything the dying person wanted so real that the people involved will often comply no matter how outrageous the request. They feel compelled to do so. People will say 'I'll never forgive myself if I don't do what he asks', and death-bed promises become sacrosanct, so that people feel they are binding in generations to come.

Having worked on providing everything the dying person needs, the next step is to prepare to say good-bye. Just as the dying person will make preparation in anticipation, so will the people around. This can find expression in 'I must get him to make a will before he dies' – a basic desire to get things sorted out – and may extend to attempts to resolve family quarrels, an anxiety that the sun should not in this case go down for ever on wrath. The relatives and friends who are left behind can also become entrapped in an over-whelming feeling that says 'I must be there when he takes his last breath'; 'I mustn't miss any last word he utters'.

This has the physical consequence of relatives and friends not being able to leave the dying person's side, in case they 'miss it'. The death-bed vigil is set up. Although this is a favourite scene in romantic fiction and melodramatic films (remember Laurence Olivier's portrayal of Lord Marchmain dying in *Brideshead Revisited*), the reality is rather different.

51

Physically and emotionally exhausted groups of people sit round the bed of the ill person feeling quite unable to leave even though they may have children at home or jobs to go to or a multitude of other functions. The vigil becomes such a powerful trap that they cannot break free from it. Conversation dries up, strain and tension increases and relatives will say that they know that the only thing that can break this living and extended nightmare is the death of the person whose bed they are sitting round, but 'What a dreadful thought to have.'

People will say that they seem to be wishing that the person would hurry up and die, but in reality it seems that this event is the only one that can break the suspended animation of events being acted out in front of them. The poignancy of having distressed relatives say, 'How many times can you say good-bye?' cannot be overestimated, and allows us a glimpse of some of the problems of anticipated grief.

Other issues that develop are concerned with caring people who wish to help relatives and friends express their grief. Many books published in the last decade or so seem to underline the importance of 'anticipatory grieving', with the result that relatives and friends can be forced into expressing emotion they may not yet be ready to express. Although it is of course true that people can be greatly helped by having the opportunity to talk about their impending loss, (both their worries about it and their wish to talk about it together with the person who is dying) this must be when the time feels right for the people involved and not when the helper, professional or lay, deems it appropriate. A lot of my work has been concerned with this area and as my experience has grown I have learnt to wait until the people involved tell me they want to talk.

Often it is our anxiety as onlookers that is the motivating force to 'get things talked about', not the wishes of those involved. Our job seems to be simply to convey a willingness to talk, and gently test out whether the people involved want to start exploring their worries and anticipated issues; but they must never be forced. A great deal of damage can be done by well-meaning people getting others to 'talk about it' or 'getting them to cry' before they are ready to do so. This can actually produce those distressing occasions when, for example, a husband and wife are sitting there looking at each other, the dying one trying very hard to get on and die because they understand everyone is waiting for them to do so, and the survivor trapped with their feelings of guilt about wishing their relative would die, whilst at the same time not being able to leave the person's side in case they miss the moment.

If we listen acutely enough, the person who is dying will tell us when the time is right. For example one person I worked with was a single parent who had five dependent children living with her, and no other adult appeared to be involved. She was being looked after at home by her children and there was a great deal of anxiety being expressed by all the carers involved as to what would happen to the children. The mother resolutely refused to talk about her diagnosis, prognosis, or future in any way. Case conferences were held, and plans were made to take the children into care and still the mother apparently obstinately refused to look at the future. However thirty-six hours before she died she telephoned for some of us to visit; she knew we had all been worried and concerned but she had it all under control. She had in fact made totally adequate arrangements for the children to be absorbed into a part of her extended family that none of us knew about. It had all been talked about by those involved. The patient knew instinctively when and how, and it all worked out as she and her children intended.

This story should not imply that there was not still a great deal of grief to be expressed by the children, but it serves to demonstrate that enforced anticipatory grief can do a great deal of harm if the timing of it is interfered with. What we as carers can do is to support the people concerned while they get on with it in their own way. For example, people with family responsibilities, when they are very ill, have very little energy to cope with anything other than their illness. It might be that we could ensure that the shopping and household chores are done, or that the children are collected from school, thus alleviating the stress of trying to cope with everyday matters whilst trying to deal with extraordinary ones. To be supporting people at a time of impending loss does not of itself mean that we have to be doing 'counselling'. Often the most useful thing we can do is something obvious and practical that other people may be overlooking in their attempt to be helpful. Relatives contemplating events after their loved one has died may then feel that they, together with the person who died, dealt with this most significant event well. Important things were said between them, plans were made and there was a prevailing sense of 'business being completed'.

This of course does not deny the grief that will be expressed, but it often acts as a strong trigger for its positive expression in a healthy way. This is the effective understanding of anticipated grief. It allows the process to start, often with the dying person having a part to play. Important feelings are shared and understood, and this can be enormously comforting to the survivors.

6 · Facing the Effects of Sudden Death and Disaster

In the last chapter we looked at some of the effects on people of knowing that a death is likely to occur and some of the anticipated grief reactions that can be recognized. Not all death is anticipated however, and death from a road traffic accident or other trauma, or the sudden onset of illness is very common. What happens to the grief reaction when there has been little warning of the impending death, or for various reasons, where there has been no opportunity to be involved in the preparation process?

As one would expect, the reaction is in some ways likely to be the opposite of what we have just described. All that has been said earlier about the need to have time to take in bad news is obviously not appropriate. The most common reaction when hearing of the sudden death of a relative or friend is to say it cannot be true! Certainly my personal reaction when hearing of the unexpected death of someone I know has always been, 'I must wait to have it confirmed in some sort of irrevocable way because I'm sure I must have got it wrong'. Certainly this caution may be justified. I once left a message on a colleague's answering machine saying that someone else could not make a meeting because she had resigned. The person for whom I had left the message replied that he was sorry to hear of the death of our mutual friend. Unravelling this startling turn of events it transpired that due to the vagaries of the recording mechanism of answering machines my original message had sounded like 'died' not 'resigned'. Leaving such miscommunications aside, though, it is still true to say that we search for confirmation, and I have found myself reluctant to make the telephone call or write the letter of sympathy in case I have heard it wrongly or been given the wrong information.

Thus when someone hears of the death of someone they are close to the reaction is, 'But it can't be true.' Often people go on to say something apparently absurd like, 'But he said he'd be home early tonight,' or 'But he never said goodbye', as though in some way the person concerned knew he was going to die. In fact people will often say that it cannot be true because they would undoubtedly have known if it was going to happen. They would have had some sort of premonition, or maybe some would say they would have had a revelation from God.

All that I have said in the last chapter about preparation and being able to sort out important issues is again not possible given this scenario. Not surprisingly this can lead to a great deal of guilt and remorse at the thought of things left unsaid, or perhaps an argument that had taken place just before the person left the house, never to return. The guilt people feel at having perhaps contributed to the illness or accident can be overwhelming. People will wonder if it is their fault that the person who died in the road traffic accident perhaps was not looking where they were going because of being preoccupied with what was happening just before they left home.

Often the survivors need proof that the person they love has actually died. This is an extension of

'Did I really hear it right?' but moves on from there, to a feeling that unless they see the evidence then they can't or won't believe it. This conjures up the picture of Thomas the disciple who refused to believe that Jesus was alive again after being killed and buried unless he could see with his own eyes the evidence of the injuries Jesus's body had received. Only then would Thomas believe. We are not talking of resurrection experiences here but of people needing to see for themselves what has been reported to them, so that the fact becomes obvious and denial or alternative explanations are less credible.

Another example of this is when someone is asked to identify a body if, for example, there has been an accident in a public place. There are, of course, civil and legal reasons for this, but it also serves the purpose of confirming to the person that their relative has actually died because they have seen it for themselves, the proof is before them. The same is true when someone has died in hospital or hospice rather unexpectedly. If the relatives are able to go to the mortuary or viewing room and be with the person who has died for as long as they feel it to be necessary, then they are more able to start absorbing the fact of their loved one's death, because again they have the evidence in front of them. They are able to say and think things, which are often very private, so as to make the event real for themselves. All this helps the grief process begin. For example, I once accompanied a daughter to the mortuary where her mother lay. The daughter went up to the body of her mother and initially started talking quietly to her, tears streaming down her face. After a few moments her voice grew louder, and she started to shout at her mother. She shouted her inner-most feelings about the hurt and anger she felt to-wards her mother who had ill-treated her a great deal when she had been young and in her mother's care. This went on for some time, but when it was finished, the daughter started crying again, this time tears of remorse, grieving for the mother who had died, and grieving for the relationship that she had never had. Being able to say these difficult, and intensely private things to her mother before the funeral was the trigger she wanted to be able to grieve genuinely and begin to feel the loss of her mother, rather than nurse the re-sentment she had had for so many years. Once we have been triggered into feeling the loss of someone who was important the grieving process is more likely to be able to start.

Another example of the importance of having time to say goodbye to the person who has died is that of a client I was working with who seemed quite unable to talk about his wife's death and seemed totally uncon-cerned that she had died tragically. He had identified her body and yet behaved as though she had never really existed. When he did acknowledge her existence he talked in dismissive and unrealistic terms. After some months of working with him it gradually emer-ged that although he had indeed identified his wife's body he had had a member of the hospital staff with him at all times. They were concerned to be caring and look after him at this time of tragedy, and he was just not really taking in what had happened.

However months later he was able to start talking about his wife and the fact that they had not been getting on for some time and had begun divorce proceedings. He felt a great deal of anger towards his wife and really wanted to express it to her but she had cheated him, as he saw it, by deliberately having an accident and dying and therefore depriving him of having the opportunity to say what he felt. Everyone around him had assumed that at the time of his wife's death he must miss her very much and said what a wonderful person she was. The opposite was true in his perception and so it was necessary to work with this widower helping him say out loud the things that he wanted to say to his wife – all the uncomplimentary and difficult things – and then, having done that, to begin grieving for the lost relationship.

If people have not had the chance to say the things they wanted to say then the sense of unfinished business can be overwhelming. The survivor finds it impossible to start expressing any feelings at all because they are so confusing, challenging and unsafe. Most people around are totally unaware that the person is likely to be having such thoughts, who in turn feels they would be deeply shocked if they knew.

Sometimes people cannot have this proof, if, for example, their loved one has been involved in an accident where the body has not been recovered. Other people avoid having this proof as a way of defending themselves against the reality of the death of the person they love. If they have not seen it for themselves then it cannot be true. It is an extreme form of the denial that we talked about earlier. It means the person never has to work through their grief, but can stay poised at a moment in time, hoping that the news they heard, but cannot believe, turns out to be wrong after all.

The picture comes to mind of Miss Havisham in Charles Dickens' *Great Expectations* sitting in her wedding dress for many years waiting for the groom who will not come. More generally we read reports of people waiting for their relative who is 'presumed dead' in some conflict or accident. Such people will often say, 'I would certainly know if he had died – I would feel it – and so I'm sure he's still alive.' Sometimes such hopes are nursed for years. It is often said in such circumstances that the shock of the news has been too great.

When I was working at a hospice I followed up bereaved people who it was felt might need some support. Usually I did this by writing to people asking if I might come and see them to find out how they were getting on. One such person who a number of us were worried about just did not answer letters or telephone calls for over a year. Some three weeks after the first anniversary of her husband's death, she telephoned saying, 'Thank you for your letter' (this being the one I had written a year earlier). 'Yes I would like you to come and see me.'

During our work with this widow, whose husband had died very unexpectedly, it turned out that since the time of his death until the time she contacted us, she had kept herself in a state of perpetual motion between her house and that of her son who lived some fifty miles away. She used the buses and wherever she found herself on the last bus at night, whether at her own home or at her son's, she would stay for the night only to set off again early the following morning. If she didn't stop to rest she didn't have to think and if she didn't think she didn't have to feel and if she didn't have to feel she didn't have to grieve the death of her husband. She did not have to accept it as real. This particular person had found the shock so great that she had not been able to acknowledge it at all except by taking this evading action.

It does seem, though, that when the death of someone we love is sudden it does not have to be that the shock is greater than when we have been expecting it. In some instances the opposite may be true. Perhaps the shock is severe enough to catapult the person into feeling all the pain and extremity of loss that their defences might not have let them do if they had had more time to get organized.

It is possible to see this most clearly when some local or national tragedy occurs. In all the shock and horror of such an incident there are usually quite a number of people involved and a sort of group mourning sets in which allows those people to react sometimes quite dramatically very quickly. When, for example, a small community experiences a tragedy in its midst, it seems that a community response quickly follows which draws people into feeling the tragedy. Think of all the people who went to the Liverpool football ground at Anfield and hung scarves and flowers on the gates of the stadium the day after the Hillsborough disaster. A sense of release is created by such public demonstrations of grief that clearly triggers many people into dealing with their feelings. It can perhaps be said that the bereavement care teams who usually now come to help at such times are the public recognition of this phenomenon. But it does need to be borne in mind that although this form of sudden death can create such instantaneous reactions there are also people who hide and keep quiet and suffer for a long time before finding the opportunity to talk to someone about their feelings or until another trigger sets them grieving.

Recently someone came to talk to me about things that had happened to him in his childhood. He said that these were things that he could not forget and he therefore wanted to try and deal with them.

Sometime after we began work he started talking about the King's Cross railway station fire that killed so many and about the fact that he was on an underground train going through the station at that time. His train had passed straight through the station and so he was safe. He had not realized the impact on him until nearly a year later he found himself shaking and crying and saying to himself, 'I was nearly killed there'. The follow-on of that being 'I wonder why I wasn't as I'm such an awful person', and hence the search for help with his past. The trigger had been the near fatality which, although in itself buried, had awakened a great deal of emotional hurt that could not be ignored and for which he was impelled to seek help. In his childhood several adults he had loved had been killed in the Second World War. Because of events at the time, his pain at these losses had not been recognized; they had been buried deep in his memory. Those memories kept him awake at night, often leaving him sweating and fearful after dreaming of long dark tunnels and falling through space. In his mind he somehow blamed himself that his relatives had died. Perhaps the child that he was when these events had occurred, had wished the adults would go away and leave him alone. The problem was that they had, but they had not come back. In his adult life all these painful thoughts had been buried but still caused a great deal of unhappiness.

It is very important that such people are helped to get back in touch with the loss that they experienced when they were young. When the losses are recognized for what they are then the healing of the pain can begin, but so often the loss is so deeply buried in people's minds that it can take a long while for it to come to the surface again. Helping people like this is sensitive work. People can feel impelled to find out what their confusion and disorientation of feeling is about, and while in this state they are vulnerable and need a great deal of skilled support.

Loss, whether recent or long ago, is very often at the bottom of our discomfiture with ourselves. If we can recognize it for what it is, then we are well on the road to dealing with it, and being able to put it behind us.

7 · Facing Multiple Grief

Sometimes the losses that we experience come so quickly one after the other that they become almost indistinguishable. We don't know which is causing the most pain or even which event grieves us the most. Multiple grief can, it seems, be experienced either over time or over events. Let's consider multiple grief over time first.

In the first chapter we looked at notions of timely and untimely grief and we saw that although the reaction to loss is the same whether or not we are expecting someone to die, the way it will be expressed does very much depend on whether it is something we might expect. For example if I am in my late fifties and I have a mother in her early eighties and she dies I will grieve for her. However, my grief will be contained within the expectation that such an event was likely to occur before too long, because of the age of my parent. If, on the other hand, I am in my early twenties and my parents are in their forties and one of them dies I will grieve in the same way, but am likely to be taken unawares and be unprepared. The unpreparedness is to do with the untimeliness not with the suddenness.

If I am unfortunate enough to experience the untimely death of several people I am attached to so that it forms something of a pattern, then I am likely to experience considerable difficulty with my bereavements: there has been none of the unconscious preparation for the death of someone close that goes on in our awareness of incidents that are likely to occur. I am not expecting my parents to be reaching the end of their life when they are fortyish but I am likely to be expecting this, although probably unconsciously, when my parents are ninetyish.

Mary was twenty-seven with two children aged eight and four. Her parents lived in another part of the country and her husband was in the army and away for long periods of time. Her mother died when Mary was eighteen, just a few weeks after she had married and moved away from home. Because of the big change in her life and all the different aspects of her new home and marriage, she did not have the opportunity to grieve her mother's death. Shortly after that her first child was born and then she had two miscarriages. Again she was a busy young mother who did not really find the time to mourn for the loss of her unborn children. The stockpile of grief continued to grow unrecognized in the business of her life, disguised by the use of prescribed and acquired sedatives and tranquillizers that she used to cope with her 'nerves'. Then her second child was born and shortly after that her father died. Again there was little chance to recognize the effect this considerable list of bereavements was having on her as she continued to take tranquillizers and look after her young children, often singlehanded. Two years after her second child was born her husband was diagnosed with a terminal illness. He remained at home where Mary nursed him until he died fifteen months later. Mary had lost both parents, her husband and two children within the space of ten years, and had not had the opportunity to acknowledge any of the effect this had on her.

Friends and neighbours saw a conscientious and hard-working mother who never seemed to sit down, and was always on the go, and kept herself to herself. Then a few weeks after her husband died Mary took a large number of pills and tried to kill herself. Some people experience too many losses at the 'not to be expected time' to the extent that the pain becomes unbearable. It can be masked for a while and often goes quite unrecognized, but there comes a time when it is not possible to disguise it and the reaction becomes an overwhelming one.

The other sort of multiple grief is that of circumstance or events. A married woman in her forties has her husband killed in an accident. This is a major and unexpected bereavement to face. If, on top of this, her income dries up because of her husband's death, if she didn't have a paid job and her husband was not insured, then her losses begin to mount up. The fact of no income may well mean that she cannot continue to pay the mortgage, and so she will have to move house thereby losing her home, friends and familiar surroundings.

The shock of all of this is so great that she might well lose her health. Then her status as a functioning person is well and truly threatened and she is bereft of much beside the loss of her husband.

In each of these circumstances the issue can often be: When do people start to grieve? Do they do it all at once, or in chronological order, or just as it seems to emerge? The advice usually is to start with the earliest one in time, especially in the circumstances of someone like Mary. Although it may seem that her greatest loss may be that of her husband, it is usually recognized that she may well be unable to look at the implications of his death until she has dealt with those that happened before he died.

In the second example it may be that the person has to deal with the surrounding bereavements before she can clear the ground enough to look at what was probably the major one. It is often noticed that when someone has a close relative die, it seems to be not unusual that the family pet dies shortly afterwards. The remaining spouse, or whoever, often seems more concerned with the death of the pet than with the death of the human being. The reason for this might be that it feels more possible to grieve the death of someone or something that is perhaps significant, but not so important as the death of the spouse. Carers and friends need to start where the person is at, and not wonder how it is that someone can seem so upset at the death of a pet and yet apparently unmoved by the untimely death of their spouse.

In the case of multiple bereavement the main issue would seem to be to try and recognize with the person how many griefs they experience and where they would want to start talking about them, rather than launch into where *we think* they should begin.

I have undertaken a lot of work with bereaved people which after a while could reach profound levels, but the first stage (which sometimes seemed never-ending) was the misery the person felt at the loss of a household object or a pet bird. I have often heard things like: 'You know, I think that bird really missed my husband. I think that's why it died.' Then you know you are about to start talking about the death of the spouse, but always through recognizing and maybe interpreting the death of the bird that was so griefstricken it died.

8 · The Death of Children and Old People

So far we have been concerned with trying to under-stand something of the general reaction people have to various forms of loss, concentrating on the reactions people will discover in themselves when they or someone close to them is dying or has died. As well as these general considerations there are particular things to bear in mind when meeting with people of certain age groups. In this chapter we will concen-trate on looking at reactions to and of dying children, and also at old people and their reaction to death. Are there any differences involved, and if there are, what are they? How can we, wanting to help look after bereaved people, be particularly aware of the needs of the very elderly or the very young, when they are coping with the impact of death and grieving on their lives.

Death and Children
Whenever one hears of a child dying, whether from disease or accident, it always seems particularly tragic. Children are seen to be innocent of life's problems and should somehow not have to face all the difficulties of death. It is often said that children have their lives before them and to die before they have had a chance to develop their personalities and lives seems particularly cruel. There is a deep sense of untimeliness about the death of a child and whereas, as we have seen in an earlier chapter, it is

possible to look on some deaths as timely and part of the natural rhythm of life, when a child is involved this does not seem to be so. Earlier we were discussing the fact that at some stages of life we are, unconsciously at least, expecting the imminent demise of someone we love, as in the case of a very elderly parent. We said that this in no way lessens the grief, but it does perhaps help us prepare for the event. In the case of the death of a child this is hardly ever the case. In a country where infant mortality is low, it is expected that children will live into adulthood and outlive their parents, so that there will not be a time when it seems likely that a child will die before their parents. The only exception to this is if the child has a disease process that has a short-term prognosis.

Talking to children who are themselves dying can obviously be very difficult. Yet it is the children themselves who often seem better able to deal with the situation. They seem to grasp its essentials and appear able to face death with remarkable courage and tenacity. Talking to them one often finds that their main priority is the adults in their lives. So such a child might say to a carer or someone they trust, 'Look after my Mummy and Daddy, please, because they are very upset. I'm going to die, but they do not want me to, and so I try to stay cheerful for them.'

Then also talking to children themselves about the death of others is a subject that adults shy away from very strongly. It will be said that children should maintain their innocence and should be protected from such distressing subjects as bereavement. So when someone in a child's life dies they are often told fabricated versions of what has happened. 'Your Mummy has gone away for a long time' usually only serves to leave the child frightened but feeling the anxiety of the adults all around which forbids further discussion. In Christian families this can be particularly so. The statement, meant to be reassuring, that 'Mummy has gone to heaven to be with Jesus', can leave the child very jealous and angry with God for taking his mother away from him. In addition the child can become very frightened, thinking that he must have been very naughty indeed for Mummy to prefer to go to be with Jesus than to stay with him. It can leave the child seeking out ways to get to heaven by bus or car. In general it can leave children with their natural curiosity expressed by the neverending 'why' questions of childhood, being squashed by the inability of adults to discuss in any other way what has really happened, and so the child learns that whatever has really happened is just too awful to be talked about. Thus children have to suppress their grief, and hold back the tears and pain. Adults, by seeking to be protective and to keep children from pain and distress, actually create it for them.

When talking with children, it is very important not to convey by trying to be gentle, that the person who has died had in any sense a choice in the matter. At some stages in their lives children are quite convinced that they have magical powers and often after a tussle about bedtime or a rejected request to watch a TV programme will 'wish' that the irritating adult would vanish. If that adult then dies the effects can be considerable. How often do parents say in exasperation, 'Oh, you'll be the death of me'? When this appears to happen literally the child may feel a guilt that can have far-reaching consequences.

Talking to children about death is a new thought for many but it can help prevent much anguish and pain if the subject is dealt with sensitively. This is particularly true if we can face doing it before they experience death for themselves, before someone in their family, maybe a grandparent, dies.

As adults we are naturally protective of children and do not want them to suffer harm. But unfortunately, in our wish to be protective, we actually create the harm we seek to protect them from. So often we give children pat, reassuring answers when we really have all sorts of unanswered questions ourselves. For a Christian it is a question of faith, but this is a profound, 'adult' question that is mystifying to children. Their natural curiosity and concretization of ideas will often give them a certainty of their own that makes much more sense. Talk to children about plants and trees and animals dying, ask them to draw their impressions of these events, and they will reveal an understanding that can leave many adults longing for a child's faith and knowledge.

A family I knew were devastated when the thirty-five-year-old mother died after a short illness. There were two children aged nine and seven and the father was determined to involve them as much as possible in talking about all that had gone on. They had helped with their mother's care when she had been at home, and taken part in planning her funeral.

One evening, shortly after the funeral, and after the supportive grandparents had returned home, Geoff, the father, sat talking to his children about how much he was missing their mother. The children listened attentively and snuggled close to their father. They said that they had been talking about it themselves. They had decided to pray to Jesus, asking that they could die too so that they could be with their Mum who they missed so much. But then they had realized that that would mean their Dad was all alone and so they had prayed again, that they could all be together in one place or the other. They then said to their Dad that although they missed their Mum very much indeed, they were beginning to see that their Dad needed them around to have people to talk to about their Mum, and so now they were asking Jesus to make sure nothing else awful happened. I remember Geoff telling me this, tears streaming down his face, marvelling at how it was his children who had the strength to carry on, and that it was they who had this practical, yet profound way of reaching to the heart of the matter.

It seems that children have not yet absorbed the fears, doubts and confusions that so often beset us as adults. Consequently they are able to face life's great issues with considerably more equanimity than people who are very much older and have a great deal of adult experience. It seems that if we as adults have the courage to talk openly and honestly to children then we have a great deal to learn from them, given their openness and ability to describe simply matters of life and death with great dignity and inbuilt wisdom. Fear is something they pick up from us adults.

Some cities in Britain are working on setting up telephone help lines for children to ring in and talk about death and their own experiences. This is because many children want to talk about the subject but cannot find an adult in whom to confide or who is willing to talk about it. There are few children who do not experience the death of a much-loved grandparent or pet when they are quite young, and yet so often they are excluded from all the changes that go on at the time of a grandparent's death, as though in some way this will leave them unaffected.

Children are often not allowed to go to funerals nor allowed to talk or ask questions about the person who has died. They are often told not to cry 'because it will upset Mummy'. All this may be done for the best of reasons but it only ensures that children bottle up their feelings as well as their tears, which, as we have seen in previous chapters, can have far-reaching effects. Grief will find an expression at some time, and if it is not allowed at the time it occurs, then it will be much more difficult to deal with when it is triggered by an event in later life. To some extent, adults can choose of their own free will whether to deal with their grief or not. Children do not have that choice, and if they are not helped by those they rely on to deal with their frightening and disturbing feelings then they can suffer considerable harm. It is undoubtedly true that when a family member dies, other members of the family are often too upset themselves to recognize the distress of the children in their midst. It may be that friends and relatives who are less affected by the death of the family member, could give some special attention to the children who are wanting to be comforted and to be told what is going on. Rather than sending the children out when the adults want to talk, it may be that a neighbour could make sure to include them in an outing to give the child time to talk to them. They could explain to the child why he feels as though the world has turned upside down and why his remaining parent seems so upset. The child needs to know that it is not his fault that everyone is so upset and that someone has died and he is not being punished. Just as the grieving adult needs tender care and attention, so does the child.

Old People dying
At the opposite end of the spectrum there are elderly people for whom death can become an all too familiar experience as their family and friends of the same age gradually die, leaving them more and more isolated. Additionally it can become something they look forward to themselves as they begin to lose their faculties and the effort of daily living becomes burdensome. However, before we go any further with this rather depressing picture it is important to underline that we are not of course talking about all people over retirement age in some blanket category of dwindling power. When talking about the elderly in this sense we are referring to people in an advanced age group of well over eighty.

At this stage there can often be many losses at the same time. Family and friends are probably dying, but there are also the losses connected with declining health, status and income. This can leave an elderly person alone and facing a bewildering number of losses at the same time. As we have seen already when we have to cope with a large number of losses in a short time, it becomes much harder to deal with the grief that we feel. Added to this is the inevitable realization of elderly people that they are less able to build new friendships, make new relationships, take on new responsibilities and tasks. It is often said that elderly people are glad to take on the role of grandparent or even great-grandparent. There's all the fun, and none of the responsibility! While this is undoubtedly true, many elderly people are not grandparents, and the lack of role can itself cause considerable grief. Much pressure can overtly or unwittingly be put on grown up children, to provide grandchildren for the delight of the grandparents.

The main difference for the very old, then, may be that whereas when they were younger it would have been possible to work through the effects of multiple grief and achieve some new balance in life, forming new relationships and so on, in old age this is less likely. The old person is more likely to experience the effects of chronic grief which are made worse by continuing life events but seldom balanced as in younger years by new attachments.

The object of bereavement work with the elderly can be more one of continuing supportive intervention and understanding the old person's need to look back over the past years and relationships than of expecting them to 'work through' their grief to its resolution. This looking back is nowadays often referred to as 'reminiscence therapy'. The idea is that if elderly people can be encouraged to think back to the times when they had lots of relationships, and when they felt they had some status and worth, then they are able to feel that status carry over more into their present life. Some of the compound loss that they feel is therefore balanced out. Old people are often a source of fascinating information and opinion about the past that young people are being taught as history! If elderly people can be involved in telling their stories as living history, especially to young people, then some sense of their real worth can return.

In some societies the elderly are revered as holders of wisdom, who often pass on, in ritualized form, information that the community needs to know. In Western society we have marginalized elderly people to a considerable extent, maybe because we place more emphasis on economic than on personal worth. Elderly people can be greatly helped if we listen to what they want to say, and receive their information as important. We can all do this – it does not require any special insights. And in the process we can help minimize the effect of compound loss in an elderly person's life.

Additionally, the elderly person often has a strong wish to tidy up, to leave things in good order. As any person gets older they naturally reflect on what the life after this one will be like and how to prepare for it. Also, in a similar way, many people, not necessarily just old people, prepare by sleeping with instructions by their bed as to what should happen to their effects if they should die during the night. Many old people in particular find it impossible to retire for the night without washing up and leaving everything tidy. Ask them why this is and they will reply that should they die during the night they do not want the person who finds them to feel they were dirty or slovenly.

Miss Barton was 87 and had been a midwife all her working life. She had been ill for some time, and gradually realized that she needed more care than could be given by the community services. She talked to people involved in her care, and it was decided that because she was becoming weak, she would be admitted to her local hospital. The ambulance arrived, but Miss Barton was not ready. She had been packed for a day or so, but had realized as she took a last look round that her fridge was still switched on with a bottle of milk inside. She said it was necessary to defrost it and turn it off before she came to hospital. She 'knew' that she would not be returning; no-one had ever seen her fridge in need of care and they weren't going to now. That went for the washed cup and saucer from the last cup of tea too. While the ambulance waited, it had to be carefully put away in the cupboard, as she had never in all her life left things draining by the sink.

However some elderly people, by contrast, have an acute wish to be left alone to die in their own surroundings with the minimum of attention. Their greatest fear is that as they become weaker, 'caring authorities' will take them over and whisk them away to be 'looked after properly'. One of the most useful things we can do is to find out from people what they would really like to happen and try to facilitate this. Too often it is us, the anxious onlookers, who want the person to be admitted to 'care' because it makes us feel better. We feel that we will be criticized if an old person is found in less than perfect conditions, and we will be thought of as neglecting them. However if this is what the old person wants, one of the most helpful things we can do is to back up their wish for this to happen.

It is necessary to stress that elderly people facing loss do not always have to be overwhelmed by their circumstances, with very little chance of preserving their dignity or sense of self-worth. It can be a real privilege to meet an older person who has experienced considerable loss in their life and has come to terms with it. Rather like the children we were discussing earlier in this chapter it is possible to meet elderly people who have achieved a serenity of understanding and/or faith that supports them utterly as they develop the skill of coming towards the end of their life.

Amy was 91 and lived alone. She was frail, and needed a lot of input from family, neighbours and community services. However she was not bitter, or depressed or withdrawn. Long conversations tired her but she loved to talk of the old days and her life as a nanny to a wealthy family. One morning when I was visiting, she said in a matter-of-fact voice, 'Jesus came to visit me last night!' Much taken aback, not least because Amy and I had had a number of conversations about her low opinion of the Church and what it stood for, I asked how she knew it was Jesus. She said, 'Well, he had a long white beard and robe of course. He told me he was just visiting to let me know he would come for me soon, but not just yet. He had one or two more jobs I was to do, to tell people things they need to know, and when that's done he'll be back. So I'm ready, and content, and I'll just wait for him.'

Unfortunately it is also true to say that suicide is very common among the elderly and it is to that subject that we now turn.

9 · Suicide and the Church's Response

Suicide is a much commoner form of death than many people suppose. It is of course a very difficult subject to talk about and many families who know or suspect that a relative has killed himself or tried to, are ashamed and refuse to talk about it, or make up all kinds of stories to cover the fact up. This is of course not always so. In some cultures it is seen as a very honourable and courageous way to die and indeed even in Western society in some remarkable circumstances the reaction is the same. When, for instance, the hero in a book or film sacrifices his life so that someone else may live, this is portrayed as extremely praiseworthy and is the subject-matter of much literature. How often is there a closing sequence in a film, with the hero facing insuperable odds, holding off the enemy, while his comrades escape. As the enemy closes in, the hero, safe in the knowledge that his comrades have made it to safety, shoots himself so that the enemy may not take him alive.

Usually though, suicide is an act of complete despair, performed by an individual who feels there is no other option, and for whom life has ceased to have any positive features. Suicide, when someone decides to take their own life by one means or another, rather than waiting to die through illness or accident, is not the same as euthanasia which may be defined as assisted death and which is a subject beyond the scope of this book.

The person trying to commit suicide has decided either rationally or whilst under extreme duress that their life is no longer bearable and that they must end it. This is often because they have such fear for the future, for some reason of their own, that death seems preferable.

For the family and friends who remain such an event is devastating. As we have discussed, the survivors need to feel involved in their loved one's dying process as much as possible. If they have been able to discuss things with the person who is dying, if there has been a time of preparation, then the shock of facing the loss caused by death is perhaps not so great. Where the cause of death is suicide this is unlikely to be so. It is essentially a private event without witnesses and often survivors feel implicated in some way. They may feel responsible for adding to the dead person's problems or may feel that if they had been more alert they would have noticed their friend's or relative's distress. They will trawl back in their minds for comments and clues that, if they had been understood at the time, might have enabled them to be more helpful. People can be left with a sense of deep confusion and blame. They will say 'I didn't know he was hoarding the tablets' or 'If only I had listened to what he was saying, maybe he was trying to tell me how he felt, and I was always too busy to listen.'

As far as the church is concerned the position is a complicated one. Remember that suicide only stopped being a crime in 1956 and until then people were imprisoned if they were found to have attempted suicide. As for burial in a churchyard or a church service for the dead person, the position is again a very complicated one. This may partly account for the secrecy and guilt that surrounds the family if their relative is understood to have taken his own life. In old churchyards it is possible to see the graves of people who have killed themselves placed beyond the walls of the burial grounds and sometimes left unmarked.

Some clergy today still take the view that a suicide victim cannot be buried in a churchyard or have a Christian funeral. This is because of the theological stance of some that people who have taken their own lives cannot go to heaven, but instead go to hell eternally because the sin is viewed as such a serious one. 'The Lord giveth and the Lord taketh away.' For some Christians the fact that we are made in God's image means that we are in some respects killing God if we attempt suicide, and so there can be no more serious sin.

The issue is a complicated one. But it is clear that if, as we have said, death from suicide is relatively common in Britain and most funeral services take place within the Christian context, then it would seem that the church needs to look at this whole subject again with a great deal more openness than has been possible up to now. In my work with church groups on the subject of bereavement, I have repeatedly found that such groups want to discuss the subject of suicide. It is of course not easy and there are few ready-made answers for a church group trying to provide bereavement care for all those with whom they come in contact, some of whom will have family members who have committed suicide.

It seems that the church could perhaps take a lead in looking at the implications of suicide, and at possible ways of providing services to try and prevent it. There may also be ways in which the church could discuss the topic more openly. It is of course a fairly familiar topic in the Bible, from Saul through to Judas – where there is enough material to offer some helpful teaching on the subject, and there is no need for it to be discussed so seldom. From open teaching on the subject can come more open discussion and from that, we can hope, a fuller understanding of the issues involved.

We have commented that people who contemplate suicide usually feel that life has nothing left to offer, and that they are a burden to themselves and those around them. The church could perhaps think how it might reach out to such people, and offer facilities and friendships that make life easier for people to face while they search for meaning in their lives.

Part III

WHAT HELP IS NEEDED?

10 · Is any Help Needed?

The bulk of this book so far has been concerned with looking at what happens when people lose something. We have talked a lot about the way grief is expressed and a little about various forms of grief. We now turn our attention to looking at what needs to be done to help grieving people. The first question that has to be asked is whether in fact anything at all needs to be done.

When talking about grief a frequent comment is, 'We never used to have this sort of fuss made in the good old days: we just had to get on with it!' What do people mean by this?

It seems to have a lot to do with how rapidly our twentieth-century world has changed, particularly in the West. Until relatively recently (some two or three generations ago) it could be said that death was a much more common experience than it is now. Mortality rates were high and many children did not survive into adulthood, whilst adulthood itself implied a much shorter lifespan than it does today. Again, we do not have room to delve into the fascinating area of population changes, but it is clearly true that in the Western world there is an older and ageing population that is radically altering the shape of the population curve. This provides many challenges of its own but here we need to look at these facts as part of the question of why handling death apparently needs more help these days. The first reason is because people experience it much less than they used to and just do not know how to react – it is beyond their experience. Many of the families I have worked with will ask, for example, how to engage the services of an undertaker because they just do not know. In previous generations the undertaker was a well-known local figure and everyone knew what to do to arrange a funeral.

The second main reason why handling grief is different these days is that death has become less and less an event that takes place within the confines of the family circle. It is more and more a high tech event where the general public and even the family concerned have little, if any, role. How often do we see a scene on television where, when some help is about to be given to a seriously ill person, the family members present are asked to wait outside. Then we see the health care professional come out of the room and say something like, 'I'm sorry, we did all we could.' People are excluded from seeing death by the fact that death has become more like an illness that must receive medical attention, rather than the last event in a person's life that they should be left in peace to deal with in whichever way they choose. If you ask medical staff how often they have seen someone die, rather than if they have been around at the time, surprisingly few will say they witnessed the actual event. All this means that individuals feel estranged and confused by an event that has very powerful consequences in their life but which they did not witness and feel very frightened of.

Third, from a sociological point of view, grief cannot be contained in the way it once was. We live in a highly mobile society where the norm is to live in small nuclear family groups, probably many miles away from the rest of the family and maybe having very little physical contact or communication with other members of the 'tribe'. This means that at a time of crisis, such as death, there are fewer people to turn to than there used to be when it was the norm to live much nearer to kinfolk. We have talked in this book about the bereaved person's need to talk and be recognized as someone having a mourning role, but if few people know us anyway, they are less likely to be aware of the major change in our life and we are less likely to feel able to talk to them about it. It is hard enough, as we have discovered, for people to know how to behave as a bereaved person. It mostly depends on other people recognizing the change that has occurred. If no one knows that this change has happened, because of the relative isolation that many people live in today, then it becomes much more difficult to grieve openly. If there are fewer people around who knew the person who has died, then there are also fewer people to notice that the person is no longer there, and there are fewer people to talk about missing him or her.

Fourth, there has been a large decline in the number of people who have an active faith of any sort, which includes an understanding of an 'afterlife'. It seems clear that one of the effects of this is that more people are fearful both for their own future and for that of the person who has died.

For these reasons it seems that it is not so much that people are making more of a fuss about bereavement these days but rather that the traditional ways of coping with it are not readily available, so that alternative ways of supporting people have to be found. Additionally it might be argued that with the almost instantaneous transmission of information we have these days, the impact of hearing about individuals or groups or communities of people dying is that much greater because we have less time to prepare for bad news. If in past decades we waited for the telegram to arrive, it did not lessen the shock, but it did prepare us for the event. Because of high media coverage we are quite likely to see tragedies as they occur including seeing people killed and the immediate stunned reactions of witnesses to ghastly events. This has to be more traumatic than if we were slowly introduced to the idea. I do not think it can be said that the manner of death is any more horrific than it used to be (although it may well be different) but it may be that the way of reporting someone's death has radically changed and that this has brought its own problems.

It is therefore suggested that it may well be necessary to provide help for certain groups of bereaved people. But it needs to be borne in mind, before we embark on the various ways of doing this, that it is by no means a universally accepted need nor is it that every bereaved person with whom we come in contact will need 'help'.

As has already been said, if the bereaved person has a supportive family or friends or somewhere like a church group where they can talk about their response to loss in an open way then this may be all the help they need. This need not mean saying how upset they are and how wonderful the dead person was.

Maybe just having the space to say all the things they want to say, including the difficult and confusing things, as often and for as long as they want to say them, is what they seek help and support with.

In most research studies of bereaved people it is recorded time and time again that, so long as the people involved have somewhere to go and someone to talk to about this major loss in their life, then they may well cope. It is a small percentage (perhaps between five and twenty per cent of bereaved people) who need more than this. In the following chapters we shall first look at some of the issues that all bereaved people need to talk about, whether it is with a friend or with the professional worker who specializes in meeting bereaved people.

11 · Practical Issues

When people think of giving help or support to those in trouble they nearly always imagine that this help will need to be of an intense and emotional nature. Visions of heavy counselling sessions come to mind and it is often felt that the grieving person must be helped to 'come to terms with it', whatever 'it' might be. Probably all of us who would like to help others make the same error.

Some twenty years ago, as a very young and inexperienced social worker, I and some colleagues working in a social services team decided that we would run a bereavement group. We made the plans and organized the publicity and on the appointed night some thirty-five people, mostly widows, turned up. After the usual social exchanges we got down to business explaining the range of counselling that we could give and the various reasons why we thought it was important to 'talk about it'. At the end of this there was a pause and gradually the widows spoke. Clearly they had misunderstood, they said. 'When they had read the publicity material offering help for the recently bereaved they had read it as an opportunity to be out and meet people again. Not to talk about their loss but to have people to go to the pub, cinema, even on holiday with. In no time my colleagues and I found ourselves organizing not counselling sessions but darts matches in the local pub circuit. Luckily I learnt early on that whereas I might see there are all sorts of emotional issues that the person grieving could work on, they may well choose not to. What is more, they really have not got the emotional energy to do this until the practical issues that beset a recently bereaved person have been sorted out.

As I have mentioned in previous chapters, at the time of a death complicated practical issues need to be decided: to bury or cremate; was there a will and if not how do you organize probate; how do you get hold of money from an account that is not in your name; how do you register a death. The list can be endless.

First, registering the death. In England and Wales this needs to be done in the area where the person died, not where they lived, if these two places are different. The Registrar is usually found at a local authority office and is the person responsible for the registration of births and marriages as well as deaths. Registration has to be done very shortly after the death itself, so the person who goes to the office to do this finds himself alongside people who are celebrating the birth of a baby, or registering a marriage. This in itself provides a complicated emotional scenario for the bereaved person to cope with. In the Registrar's office there are forms to be filled in and information to be provided. Facts such as the deceased woman's maiden name, the birthplace of the deceased and so on will all be needed, as will the person's national insurance number, state benefit books and NHS card. Whoever goes to register the death is referred to as the person 'responsible for the disposal of the deceased' and is given a range of forms including the death certificate, the form that the undertaker needs to have as authorization to proceed, and another form relating to benefits available. If the family has decided on cremation, the undertaker will need a further form, so this decision needs to have been made prior to the visit to the Registrar.

I have gone through this procedure in some detail, not so much as a practical guide as to how to make the arrangements, but to demonstrate how much practical activity surrounds someone's death. Details and procedures change, of course, with alterations in the law, and different countries have different systems.

We have not mentioned what happens if the cause of death is unknown and inquests or autopsies have to be carried out; or if the deceased person wanted to donate organs; if they wanted to be buried in another country, and so on. The reason behind all of the red tape even under normal circumstances is that a legal process is being implemented. The state has to be assured that the person being disposed of is the person others say he is, that the manner of his dying can be explained and is legally acceptable. Much of the legislation harks back to the time when individuals were less readily identifiable than they are nowadays and so protection was necessary to ensure that foul play was not involved.

Whatever the reasons for this procedure the effect is to involve family and friends in a welter of activity that they were probably unprepared for. Some say this is in fact useful because it keeps people busy at a time when, as we have seen, it is probably too painful to have time on your hands to sit and reflect.

Decisions about burial or cremation may be clear cut. If, as we have suggested, those closest to the person who has died have had the opportunity to discuss what should happen, maybe with the person himself, and their wishes are known, then the decision has already been made and it is a united one. If the dead person has left instructions about the arrangements then this can be a helpful thing. When the issue has not been discussed because it is felt to be too painful to talk about or because it is considered an unsuitable topic of conversation, then there may be problems. Families find that they have differing views and that these are very strongly held, because of course of the emotional nature of the decision being made. Families may be split and huge rifts created if it is felt that the wrong choice has been made. For some religious convictions will dictate the manner of disposal, but again these may not be shared by everyone involved. So an important decision has to be made in a hurry by people who are clearly affected by the events of the last few days. I would therefore urge people to try and talk about these kinds of things before the situation arises because this can avoid so much misery later on.

There are still more practical decisions to be made, concerning, for example, the kind of coffin or casket or rose tree or commemorative plaque; whether to have flowers or not; how much to spend. The cost of a funeral or cremation is considerable and many people have the feeling that the dead person should have the very best, but this decision can put them in debt for some time to come. In ordinary circumstances the family contemplating spending a considerable amount of money would probably spend some time shopping around getting quotations. This all seems rather difficult to do when arranging a funeral or cremation, and anyway adds to the practical load.

One of the most common practical problems at the time of someone's death is that there are lots of extra expenses involved and yet it is not possible to get hold of cash or obtain access to funds because financial accounts have to be reorganized following the death of the person concerned. If the wishes of the dead person are known, namely if he has made a will, the process will be easier, but it will still take some time to go through all the necessary procedures. If the person has not made a will then the process usually takes a good deal longer which may mean that a whole range of practical issues are held in abeyance whilst the situation is resolved. Disposal of property or effects all have to wait until it is formally decided who has the task of doing this. Again, the importance of leaving a formally constructed will cannot be overestimated. The view that many people have, of 'I haven't got anything and anyway it all goes to my wife', can often lead to legal difficulties and may not be so straightforward as is supposed.

When someone dies, then, there is a vast range of practical decision-making to be done by people who, as we have said, are likely to be shocked and in a state of indecision. This practical load continues with issues like disposing of the clothes of the person who has died. Very commonly people decide to move house, redecorate, change their job and, in many different ways, wipe out the past which has become so painful. We will discuss a little later the emotional implications of this but for the moment we are reflecting on the practical issues that overwhelm the bereaved person. Some things need to be attended to very quickly because of the changed circumstances; others, because they provide a refuge from 'thinking about things', keep people occupied and thus leave no time for speculation or for unhappy thoughts to flood in.

So when we are thinking about helping bereaved people, instead of turning to emotional issues straightaway, we should perhaps consider the practical issues that the bereaved person is facing. When he or she is perhaps overwhelmed by events, offers of practical help may be exactly what the person could do with, rather than being asked to confront difficult emotional reactions. It seems that this is particularly true in the early stages of bereavement when so much has to be reorganized. A little later on, when all the relatives have gone home and the number of attentive friends at the time of the funeral has dwindled, it might be the time when the bereaved begin to reflect on their changed circumstances and try to evaluate how they feel both about themselves and the person who has died.

Meantime anyone wishing to help can offer to do the shopping, cleaning, washing and ironing – all the things that a bereaved person just cannot be bothered with. A little later on offers of company on a regular basis, or arranging visits to mutual friends, or invitations to a meal, can be enormously useful. The bereaved person feels included and wanted, and even if invitations are repeatedly turned down, as they might well be, this does not mean that they are not deeply appreciated.

12 · Emotional Issues

Bereaved people trying to make sense of what has happened to them often find that one of the most difficult things is to discover that they 'cannot think straight' and when they do their thoughts are often so disturbing and frightening that they feel they've 'gone mad'.

Mr and Mrs Ware were in their mid-thirties with children aged thirteen and ten. They were both in banking, and were therefore used to making quick decisions and to having a lot of responsibility. Then Mr Ware became terminally ill and died some six months after diagnosis. Mrs Ware telephoned me five weeks after her husband died saying that she felt her children should be taken into care and she should be hospitalized because she could no longer cope. When I asked why this was so she explained that since her husband died she had been managing well and felt that she had coped with all the trauma. However, that morning she had found herself pre-paring the children's sandwiches for school – as she did each day – by buttering newspaper instead of the bread. This had to mean, she felt, that she had gone mad because, as she saw it, there could be no other explanation.

People who are used to having responsible jobs at home or in the office and who are known to be good managers and organizers cannot understand why suddenly the simplest task seems to be beyond them, and this makes them feel out of control and very unsafe. The emotional help that we can offer most directly to bereaved people is to explain that such behaviour is not an indication that they have gone mad, but in fact rather the opposite. It is the way that our feelings tell us that they have got too much to cope with at the same time and they need some help – in the jargon this is called needing some 'ventilation'. So strange behaviour is an indication of stress. If you like, it is the same as the body producing the symptom of a cough when the lungs have become congested and need to get rid of the secretions in them. The cough is there to signal that something is going awry and needs attention after which it will be all right. When we find ourselves unable to think straight the pattern is the same. Our emotions are saying they are under a lot of stress and are needing some help.

The help that is needed is essentially for someone to listen, maybe repeatedly and sometimes, it seems, endlessly. It is for someone to support the person whilst they try to unravel their thoughts in such a way that it becomes clear that they can say anything, no matter how bizarre or odd it sounds, because that will be the way they sort out their feelings in order to cope with them. It is not that people need to change or be 'cured'; it is that they need to pursue their thoughts to their logical conclusion and from there make decisions on the basis of what they have discovered about themselves. This can take a lot of time as it must proceed at the person's own pace and not fit within the time span that the helper finds convenient or thinks sufficient.

In the course of such conversations it often happens that the bereaved person is not only troubled by thoughts that they might be going mad but by the notion that they are very bad. This usually has to do with the guilt they feel connected with the death, or the shame they feel at their anger and resentment towards the one who has left them. This might be because they were estranged in some way before the person's death or because they resent the person dying and leaving them to cope. Again this is a common and 'normal' reaction, but many people feel so ashamed of thoughts like these that they hardly dare express them unless they feel safe enough to do so and trust the person they are talking to sufficiently for such a revelation to seem acceptable.

One of the most important aspects of bereavement help is perhaps enabling a grieving person to talk about their negative thoughts as well as their sad thoughts (which are the ones it is presumed we want to hear). It is often useful for the helper to introduce the notion of the normality of having both difficult and sad thoughts about the deceased person and then from there the bereaved person can pick up the conversation if he or she wants to do so.

At some stage a bereaved person usually begins to feel that he or she must be very selfish indeed. Here they are, recently bereaved, and yet all they can think is 'What about me?' – when surely they should be thinking instead about the person who has died. It is at this stage that we can perhaps be of most use by pointing out that that is mostly what grief is about. We mourn the loss of the person who died and we respond to the change that this effects in our lives with panic or elation or anxiety or a whole gamut of emotions that may take us by surprise. That is why it is possible for a Christian in particular to feel at one and the same time joyful because the person who has died has entered eternal life, and overwhelmingly sad, or guilty, or relieved at the thought that they have died and the survivor is left with vast changes to absorb into their life pattern.

The emotional help that we can give is often about unravelling this complex package of emotion into a process that can be gently reviewed and understood by the person feeling it all. Again it is crucial to stress that this can be a lengthy process taking some months or years depending on circumstances, availability of help and a number of other variables.

In a few instances the loss of someone close can propel the survivor into an overwhelming emotional whirlpool that cannot be contained without expert help or hospitalization or treatment or a combination of all of these. Often this is to do with the fact that the current bereavement has driven the person into emotional overload because of everything else that is happening in their life either currently or over a period of time. Mercifully the number of people who suffer to this extent is small and their need for help is usually recognized by those with whom they come into contact.

13 · Social Issues

One of the commonest problems of bereavement is that of feeling isolated and alone and having no one to turn to. This is obviously true whether the bereavement is caused by death or separation or change of circumstances.

Mrs Ireland had been married for thirty-nine years. She had two grown-up children who were both married and living away from home. Her husband began to complain of headaches and lethargy and after a period of investigation in hospital it was discovered that he had a malignant cerebral tumour. Sadly he deteriorated very quickly until he could no longer care for himself or communicate in any understandable way. Mrs Ireland, in tears, explained that her situation was of course an awful one. She loved her husband dearly. The most dreadful part, as she saw it though, was her complete inability to discuss the situation with her husband. She said that throughout their married life they had always talked things through and come to decisions between them about what to do. She found herself walking along the road saying 'I'll talk it all over with Alan when I get in – he'll know what to do', only to remember that it was Alan who was the cause of the heartache. He could not join in the discussion. This time Mrs Ireland had to make her decision alone and that was horrendously difficult to do, especially as it involved deciding about the future care of her husband.

The loneliness that bereaved people feel can be intense. It can be explained by the fact that so much of Western life in the later part of the twentieth century is geared to groups and families, partnerships and couples. In the supermarket packs of food are seldom in single-portion size but are much more likely to be in family economy packs. Visits to hotels or theatres, going on holiday or to restaurants are all difficult things to do on one's own, and if they are undertaken, people may have to pay more or end up in a corner, marginalized and away from the main clientèle. This sort of treatment of course reinforces the sense of isolation and loneliness. So many bereaved people, especially women, do not continue to try and have a social life as it is just too difficult and usually just serves to reinforce their sense of isolation and hurt. Widows will talk of being acutely aware of the gap by their side when they are used to being viewed as one of a couple (obviously couples who divorce or separate feel the same). Often in the married couple's social life, it would be one member of that partnership who was the particular friend of, say, another couple. If that person dies the remaining friends are not sure whether to keep up the contact or not. Similarly, if parents lose a daughter, do they maintain contact with their erstwhile son-in-law if he marries again, or was their contact really only through their daughter?

Bereaved men often talk about their social problems being rather more connected with their homes than outside them. They explain that they have always fended for themselves because of being at work, but when it comes to going home the difficulties begin. The house that always used to be warm and welcoming when they got home is now dark and cold. There is no meal ready; all the washing and ironing sits there waiting to be done, instead of clean clothes waiting to be worn again. Many men feel a very great sense of despair and discomfort upon entering what used to be their home with their wife, but what is now a house that seems to demand a lot of time-consuming work. Clearly with greater parity between the sexes the rather traditional view painted here of women afraid to go out and men afraid to go home may be less typical, but the main point remains.

The sort of help that can be offered here is of course manifold. Bereaved people may seem reluctant to accept invitations out, but that is often because they feel that they will be in the way or make an odd number at any gathering, and the hurt and embarrassment this creates is awful. If invitations can be issued sensitively and with thought then they will be much appreciated by the recipient. Inclusion in group activities is important as is, particularly, the opportunity for friends to be in the home of the bereaved person not just for 'heavy conversation' but also for social exchange.

When someone is bereaved they have to make considerable readjustment socially speaking. Their tax and insurance status changes. They have to rely on doing everything for themselves rather than sharing the tasks. Someone recently said to me 'I'm gradually getting over the death of my husband, but if I had realized all the extra work I would have I'm not sure I could have coped. Now I have a salaried job instead of running the home I have no time to do the shopping, take the car to the garage or wait in for service engineers of various sorts. It takes more than one person to run a household.' I'm sure we all know what she meant!

So we are talking in general terms about being willing to share our time, energy, space and care, particularly with people who have been recently bereaved through some major form of loss, maybe for a short period of time while they readjust, maybe for a long time as the person or people involved learn to face life's vicissitudes alone.

Christians will see in this the biblical command to 'look after the widows and the orphans' and it seems that churches are uniquely placed to provide this sort of support. One of the things that can emerge is a great deal of mutual help, so that there is not just one group of people giving out to another but a group of people reaching out to one another. What churches can do well is to provide the location, the opportunity and the safety for people to explore the formation of new relationships and new beginnings.

Bereaved people do not always need to be 'done unto'. Very often they just need the opportunity to meet other people in a similar situation, and in so doing learn to form new relationships again, but in a safe and caring atmosphere.

14 · Spiritual Help

In the library of bereavement literature there is a vast range of material on the topic of spiritual help for the bereaved. Often this takes the form of providing comforting words from the Bible and many Christian societies also publish tracts and pamphlets on the subject. If these are thought to be appropriate for the person you are going to be in touch with, then the local Christian bookshop will undoubtedly stock a range. It is very true that the written word can so often reach people more easily than the spoken word can do.

In addition, at a time of bereavement many people ask searching questions of the 'why should it happen to me?' variety. They not infrequently turn for some answers to the religion that they may have been introduced to in the past but have long since rejected. We spoke in earlier chapters of people's search for meaning as they look for the person who has died, and saw that at such times a sortie into faith healing or clairvoyance is quite common.

As we said in the last chapter, the Church is well placed to give a positive message at this time, to speak of how mortality is understood and how it fits in with the Christian message of salvation. Being able to speak of this with compassion and understanding requires wisdom. For example a bereaved person may well ask that as their relative who died was not a Christian, does this mean that he or she has not 'gone to heaven'? Does it mean that the survivor will never see them again in whatever sort of afterlife they envisage? I have heard Christians give all sorts of response to this, for some will feel that indeed a non-Christian will not attain to eternal life. Other believing people will say that they really cannot answer in that way because it does not seem to fit with other messages in the New Testament of people being held to account 'in the latter days'.

An interpretation I have often heard is that God's ways are mysterious and wonderful, and it may well be that in the very last moments of the person's life they had an encounter with God that set them on the path to eternal life. We should not limit the power and majesty of God to what we can understand but leave it to him.

Perhaps it can be said that, when people are searching for meaning, they are at the beginning of a journey, not at the end of it. The problem with producing absolutes, or trite answers for grieving people who are asking questions, is that they feel defeated before they have begun to explore. I know very little about gardening, but I am keen to learn more, as I develop my garden. If kind friends talk to me in jargon, using Latin names for all the plants, and immediately discussing the Ph-value of my soil, I am likely to give up. I do not understand what they are talking about, and I do not have the knowledge to take up their suggestions.

People concerned about their recently deceased relative or friend are rather like me in my garden. They need a sympathetic response, that is understandable and starts at the beginning. Complicated theological issues like salvation and redemption need to be talked through carefully, and at the hearer's own pace, for then they will hear. It needs to be related to their own experience, for then they will understand.

The spiritual care of the bereaved demands a book all on its own and we cannot do it justice here since we have been more concerned with the human experiences that people undergo. What is clear, though, is that the bereaved have a special place in God's kingdom and this should be reflected in his church so that bereaved people can feel that they have at least one known place where they can feel at home. When life seems strange, uncertain and frightening, the church should provide a sanctuary from which emanates understanding, support and the possibility of new attachments in all their variety and hope for the future.

Suggested Further Reading

Bowlby, J., *Separation, Attachment and Loss* Vols I–III *Loss,* Penguin 1981.

CIO Publications, *Funerals and Ministry to the Bereaved,* 1985.

Green, Wendy, *Gran's Grave,* Lion 1989.

Hollings, Michael, *Alive to Death,* Mayhew-McCrimmon 1976.

Jackson, Edgar, *Understanding Grief,* SCM 1985.

Kübler-Ross, Elisabeth, *Living with Death and Dying,* Souvenir Press 1982.

Parkes, C.M., *Bereavement,* Penguin 1975.

Pincus, Lily, *Death in the Family,* Faber 1976.

Shaw, Luci, *God in the Dark: Through Grief and Beyond,* Highland Books 1989.

Smith, Carole, *Social Work With the Dying and Bereaved,* Macmillan 1982.

Speck, Peter, and Ainsworth-Smith, Ian, *Letting Go: Caring for the Dying and Bereaved,* SPCK 1982.

Whitaker, Agnes (ed.), *All in the End is Harvest* (an anthology), Cruse/DLT 1984.

Wiebe, Katie, *Alone: A Search for Joy,* Hodder Christian Paperbacks 1989.

Williams, Donna Reilly and Sturzl, JoAnn, *Grief Ministry: Helping Others Mourn,* Resource Publications, Inc. 1990.

Worden, W., *Grief Therapy and Grief Counselling,* Tavistock Publications 1983.

Wynnejones, Pat, *Children, Death and Bereavement,* Scripture Union 1986.

Some Useful Addresses

National Self-Help Clearing House
  Graduate School and University Center / CUNY
  Room 610, 25 West 43rd St.
  New York, NY 10036
  212-642-2944
  (has listings from all states for help in grief)

THEOS Foundation (They Help Each Other Support)
  1301 Clark Bldg.
  717 Liberty Ave.
  Pittsburg, PA 15222
  (help for widows)

NAIM
  U.S. Catholic Conference
  Family Life Division
  721 N. La Salle Dr.
  Chicago, IL 60610
  312-844-1286

National Sudden Infant Death Foundation
  10500 Little Patuxent Pkwy.
  Suite 420
  Columbia, MO 21044
  301-964-8000

Victim Services Agencies
  210 Joralemon St.
  Room 608
  Municipal Building
  Brooklyn, NY 11201
  718-834-6688
  (help for families of homicide victims)

Parents Without Partners
  8807 Colesville Rd.
  Silver Spring, MD 20910
  301-588-9354

American Association of Suicidology
  2459 S. Ash
  Denver, CO 80222
  303-692-0985
  (help for friends and families of suicides)

The Compassionate Friends
  P.O. Box 3696
  Oakbrook, IL 60522-3696
  312-990-0010
  (help in the death of a child)

AARP (American Association of Retired Persons)
  (need not be member)
  Widowed Persons Services
  Joan Gibala (Public Relations)
  601 E. St. N.W.
  Washington, DC 20049
  202-434-2260
  (help in the death of a spouse)

National Association of Uniform Services, Inc.
  Society of Military Widows
  5535 Hempstead Way
  Springfield, VA 22151
  703-750-1342

National Funeral Directors Association
  11121 W. Oklahoma Ave.
  Milwaukee, WI 53227
  414-541-2100

Concerns of Police Survivors, Inc.
  9423 A / Marlboro Pike
  Upper Marlboro, MD 10772
  301-599-0445

National Hospice Organization
  901 N. Moore St.
  Suite 901
  Arlington, VA 22209
  703-243-5900
  (help in cancer deaths)

Parents of Murdered Children and Other Survivors
  100 E. 8th St., B-41
  Cincinnati, OH 45202
  513-721-5638

Displaced Homemakers Association
  —New Beginnings
  1411 K Street, Suite 930
  Washington, DC 20009
  202-628-6767
  (help for women newly widowed or divorced)